Opening up
Luke’s Gospel

GAVIN CHILDRESS

DayOne

'There are no greater books in all the world than the four Gospels. And there is no better way for the newcomer to learn of Jesus Christ than to read through one of them as it introduces the God-man, not in abstract theories but in the encounters and conversations of everyday life. Gavin Childress has written a clear guide to Luke's Gospel that is well-suited to assist the first-time reader through what may be strange territory, explaining its setting in history and in the whole Bible, and—even more—bringing Jesus near to the issues and concerns of today.'

John Nicholls,
CEO, London City Mission

First printed 2006

ISBN 978-1-84625-030-9

British Library Cataloguing in Publication Data available

Published by Day One Publications
Ryelands Road, Leominster, HR6 8NZ
Telephone 01568 613 740 FAX 01568 611 473

email—sales@dayone.co.uk
web site—www.dayone.co.uk
North American—e-mail—sales@dayonebookstore.com
North American web site—www.dayonebookstore.com

Designed by Steve Devane and printed by Gutenberg Press, Malta

To Keith Johns:
Once he was my schoolteacher;
now a wise friend and fellow pastor

List of Bible abbreviations

THE OLD TESTAMENT

Gen.	Genesis	1 Chr.	1 Chronicles	Dan.	Daniel
Exod.	Exodus	2 Chr.	2 Chronicles	Hosea	Hosea
Lev.	Leviticus	Ezra	Ezra	Joel	Joel
Num.	Numbers	Neh.	Nehemiah	Amos	Amos
Deut.	Deuteronomy	Esth.	Esther	Obad.	Obadiah
Josh.	Joshua	Job	Job	Jonah	Jonah
Judg.	Judges	Ps.	Psalms	Micah	Micah
Ruth	Ruth	Prov.	Proverbs	Nahum	Nahum
1 Sam.	1 Samuel	Eccles.	Ecclesiastes	Hab.	Habakkuk
2 Sam.	2 Samuel	S.of.S.	Song of Solomon	Zeph.	Zephaniah
1 Kings	1 Kings	Isa.	Isaiah	Hag.	Haggai
2 Kings	2 Kings	Jer.	Jeremiah	Zech.	Zechariah
		Lam.	Lamentations	Mal.	Malachi
		Ezek.	Ezekiel		

THE NEW TESTAMENT

Matt.	Matthew	Gal.	Galatians	Heb.	Hebrews
Mark	Mark	Eph.	Ephesians	James	James
Luke	Luke	Phil.	Philippians	1 Peter	1 Peter
John	John	Col.	Colossians	2 Peter	2 Peter
Acts	Acts	1 Thes.	1 Thessalonians	1 John	1 John
Rom.	Romans	2 Thes.	2 Thessalonians	2 John	2 John
1 Cor.	1 Corinthians	1 Tim.	1 Timothy	3 John	3 John
2 Cor.	2 Corinthians	2 Tim.	2 Timothy	Jude	Jude
		Titus	Titus	Rev.	Revelation
		Philem.	Philemon		

Background

Why another Gospel?

Why do we have four Gospels? Would the world be a worse place if there were no Gospel of Luke? Some might feel that *one* biography of the Lord Jesus would be enough. By way of analogy, we see depth in creation around us because we have two eyes and a brain that puts the two images together. Thus we see in three dimensions! The Gospels reveal Jesus not from three, but four viewpoints. Each one gives us a slightly different perspective on the life of the Saviour. Together, these perspectives give us the fullest and most complete picture of the Son of God.

The Author

A reader of Luke's Gospel will quite reasonably ask, 'Who was Luke and why did he write this?' Luke was not among the twelve disciples of the Lord. We know that he was a doctor. In Colossians 4:14, Paul called him 'the beloved physician'. He probably came to faith during one of Paul's missionary journeys. In the Acts of the Apostles (also written by Luke), we discover that the author seems to have lived near to Troas in Asia Minor (Acts 16). Luke trusted in the Lord Jesus, and began to accompany Paul. In the Acts of the Apostles, Luke enters his own narrative but then, quite suddenly (in Acts 16:10-17), the reader encounters the word 'we' in describing Paul's travels,

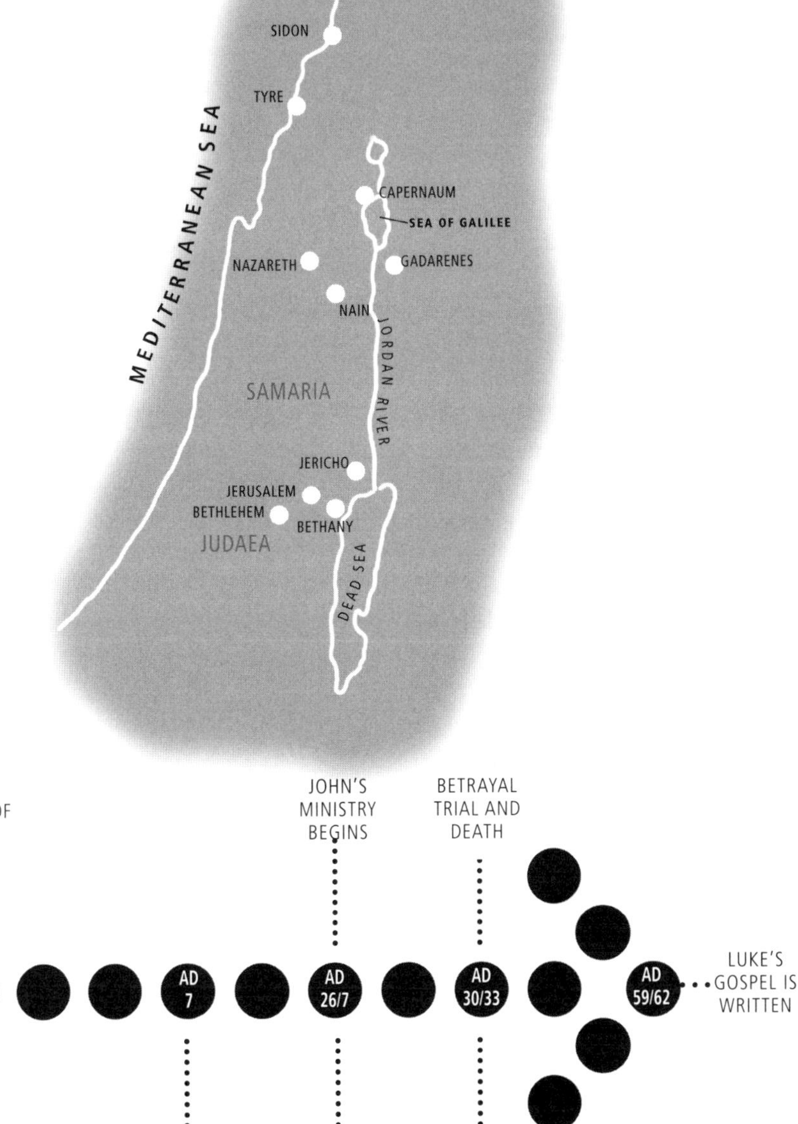
SIDON
TYRE
MEDITERRANEAN SEA
CAPERNAUM
SEA OF GALILEE
NAZARETH
GADARENES
NAIN
JORDAN RIVER
SAMARIA
JERICHO
JERUSALEM
BETHLEHEM
BETHANY
JUDAEA
DEAD SEA
IRTH OF JESUS
JOHN'S MINISTRY BEGINS
BETRAYAL TRIAL AND DEATH
5 BC
AD 7
AD 26/7
AD 30/33
AD 59/62
LUKE'S GOSPEL IS WRITTEN
IRTH OF OHN THE BAPTIST
JESUS' VISIT TO THE TEMPLE AGED 12
JESUS' MINISTRY BEGINS
RESURRECTION AND ASCENSION

indicating that Luke had joined the apostle Paul.

Luke provides a very full picture of the life of Christ, setting out material from eyewitnesses and applying painstaking attention to detail (see 1:3). We know that, when writing the Acts of the Apostles, Luke took great care to get historical, political and geographical details right. We can therefore be confident that the same scrupulous accuracy has been applied as Luke wrote his Gospel. Let us learn to trust our Bibles!

Luke seems not only to have been a painstakingly accurate historian, but a faithful believer and loyal friend, as is evident from the writings of Paul. The apostle wrote his second letter to Timothy as he prepared to stand before Caesar, approaching the end of his life. Having spoken with a broken heart of so many brothers who deserted him when he most needed them, he writes, 'Only Luke is with me' (2 Tim. 4:11).

Introducing the Gospel of Luke

The Gospel of Luke gives us a large amount of material not found in the other Gospels. Of the total 1,151 verses in this Gospel, 499 are found only here. Of these, 261 are the sayings of Jesus. If there were no Gospel of Luke, we would have none of the following:

Some parables found only in Luke

The Good Samaritan; The Rich Fool; The Barren Fig Tree; The Wedding Banquet; The Prodigal Son; The Dishonest Steward; The Rich Man and Lazarus; The Persistent Widow; The Pharisee and the Publican; The Ten Pounds (or 'minas')

Some accounts found only in Luke

Zacharias and Elizabeth (1:5-80); The birth of John the Baptist (1:57,58); The shepherds of Bethlehem (2:8-20); The widow of Nain's son (7:11-17); The seventy sent out (10:1-12); Mary listening as Martha served (10:38-42); Ten lepers healed (17:11-19); Zacchaeus (19:1-10); The dying thief who believed (23:39-43)

1 Luke Chapter 1

The Gospel is written to Theophilus, whose name means 'friend of God'. From this name we can instantly connect this book to the Acts of the Apostles, a book which is also addressed to Theophilus (Acts 1:1), and also written by Luke.

The prologue (1:1-4)

The opening verses reveal that the author was fully aware of other writings of the life of Jesus. He speaks of 'many' who have written of him (v. 1). Luke makes it clear that his Gospel is in no way written to challenge the events as recorded by others, but that he wished to write them in strict chronological order. He writes to confirm the certainty of the things that were already believed.

John's birth announced (1:5-25)

As if to emphasize that this Gospel contains unique material, the first twenty-five verses are found nowhere else. Luke takes us back to the time before John the Baptist was conceived, and introduces us to his parents. Zacharias and Elizabeth were a devout couple who were unable to have children. Childlessness can cause tremendous secret grief. In biblical times these feelings were compounded by the fact that the community set a great emphasis on childbearing (see v. 25).

Zacharias was a priest and therefore served in the Temple. Herod the Great had constructed, at unimaginable expense, this remarkable edifice. It covered some thirty-five acres. Zacharias had to take it in turns with other priests to conduct the public worship of God and pray for the nation. One day he was offering incense before God. That very moment the Lord answered the prayers of many years. He would have a son.

The promise (1:11-20)

The angel Gabriel appeared and told Zacharias that the child was to be called John, which means 'Jehovah has been gracious'. God was performing a miracle of grace in the life of this couple. John must live as a Nazirite, that is, an Israelite especially consecrated to God. Such a person was forbidden to drink wine or even grape juice, so that all his strength and joy would be seen to come from God alone, and not from alcohol.

In erse.17, the angel clearly links John to the last verse of the Old Testament. Here we see the unity and continuity of the Bible, and that John's ministry would fulfil the final promise of the Hebrew Scriptures (Mal. 4:5, 6).

Zacharias was unsure. In verse 20 the angel Gabriel told him that he would be unable to speak until *after* John was born, because, 'you did not believe my words'. We see here the importance of trusting in the power of God to do the impossible (see v. 37). Doubt is always a stain upon one's character, and God regards questioning his word as a sin rather than merely a weakness.

The days that followed (1:21-25)

Subsequently a very unusual situation arises: a husband unable to speak, and his wife, Elizabeth, though long past childbearing age, expecting a baby and living in seclusion from the world. In a sense Elizabeth's isolation was just the right prelude for the life of John the Baptist himself. He would one day live far from the multitudes in the wilderness, hearing the voice of God, surrounded by the deep silence of the desert.

FOR FURTHER STUDY

1. Angels are described in Scripture as beings that 'excel in strength' (Ps. 103:20, see also 2 Kings 19:35). How have people reacted to the sight of angels? Consider Jacob at Bethel (Gen. 28:12-17) and the shepherds of Bethlehem (Luke 2:9).
2. See 1:26-38. Look up and read in context the following references to the angel Gabriel: Daniel 8:16, 9:21.
3. Consider the life of a Nazirite (Num. 6:1-21). What came first in his life? Note how different such a man's priorities were from our own!

TO THINK ABOUT AND DISCUSS

1. Zacharias and Elizabeth belong to a long list of holy couples in the Bible who were childless at the beginning, but who were later blessed with children: Abraham and Sarah, Jacob and Rachel, Manoah and his wife (the parents of Samson), Hannah and Elkanah (the parents of Samuel). What do you think they learned from being tested in this way?
2. See Luke 1:20. Zacharias was unable to speak because of his unbelief. Why does God rebuke doubt? (See Matt. 14:29-31, Mark 16:14 and John 16:7-9.)
3. See Luke 1:15. Why is being filled with the Holy Spirit closely linked to having control over alcohol? (See Eph. 5:18.)
4. What does Luke 1:15 tell us about the possibility of young children knowing God?
5. What effect might it have upon your character if you were struck silent for many months?

Christ's birth announced (1:26-38)

Elizabeth had a cousin whose life was to change dramatically. This godly young woman, Mary, met the angel Gabriel. She was engaged to be married to a carpenter named Joseph. In biblical times, such a relationship was considered as binding as marriage itself; a broken engagement was seen as a kind of divorce.

A comparison of Matthew 1 and Luke 3 shows that both Mary and Joseph were descendents of King David, who reigned some 950 years earlier. The true royal succession had ended centuries before, and the Herods had usurped the throne. This is why Mary and Joseph were poor. Descent from King David was a fact recognized more than once during our Lord's ministry, some referring to him as 'son of David' (see Luke 18:38). As such, he was lawful heir to the throne of Israel. Scripture declares him the 'King of kings and Lord of lords' (Rev. 19:16).

Now it is some months since Elizabeth conceived. Mary is told by the angel that she is 'highly favoured' and 'blessed among women' (v. 28). Gabriel's message begins by focusing on her child, Jesus, soon to be conceived. His greatness and glory are described (vv. 31-33). He will sit on the throne of David, yet be infinitely greater, because his kingdom will never end (v. 33).

Gabriel describes the immense power involved in bringing this about (v. 35). Mary is also informed of Elizabeth's pregnancy. In reacting to all this overwhelming information Mary does not question God's power or his choice, but rather says, 'Behold the maidservant of the Lord! Let it be to me according to your word' (v. 38). If only every one of us were so willing to obey the voice of God!

Mary does not question God's power or his choice, but rather says, 'Behold the maidservant of the Lord! Let it be to me according to your word.'

Mary visits Elizabeth (1:39-45)

The saying 'a joy shared is a joy doubled' was certainly true for Mary and Elizabeth. They were first cousins, and therefore John the Baptist and Jesus Christ would be related as second cousins. Mary travelled seventy or eighty miles south to the city of Judah where Elizabeth lived. On arriving, sensing the proximity of the unborn Christ in Mary's womb, Elizabeth's son leaped within her. At that point Elizabeth was filled with the Holy Spirit (vv. 41, 44). There is no sense of competition between the women as to whose son was the greatest. Instead, Elizabeth bursts forth in spontaneous praise of the Lord Jesus, her Messiah (vv. 42, 43).

FOR FURTHER STUDY

1. Suggest why Mary, a young woman, was less doubting than Zacharias, an elderly and well-established priest.
2. Mary is called 'blessed among women' (v. 42). Is this because of her own purity or because of the blessings granted to her?
3. The Holy Spirit filled Elizabeth as Mary arrived. Look up the following two occasions when the Holy Spirit came in power and consider how often in the Bible he seems to come at an unexpected moment: 1 Samuel 19:20-24; Acts 2:1, 2.

TO THINK ABOUT AND DISCUSS

1. Would we feel 'highly favoured' (1:28) or 'highly fearful' if God had some special task for us? Are we willing to do whatever he asks?
2. John the Baptist and Jesus were related. Of the twelve disciples of the Lord, six were brothers. What does this tell us about God's view of family ties?
3. Mary had learned the lesson of obedience (v. 38). Later, she told servants at the wedding in Cana, 'Whatever he says to you, do it' (John 2:5). Have we learned this lesson?

The song of Mary (1:46-56)

This song is the outpouring of praise from a humble heart. When we think of how many people have tried to make Mary almost a goddess ('Queen of Heaven'), this song reveals that her focus is not on herself, but on the blessings granted to her. Her opening words are beautiful: 'My soul magnifies the Lord, and my spirit has rejoiced in God my Saviour…' (v. 46). Mary wanted God to have all the praise. Some have claimed that, in order to give birth to the Lord Jesus, Mary must have been without sin. Yet she calls God her 'Saviour', thus recognizing that she herself was a sinner whom God had saved.

Mary's song introduces us to the saving work of the Lord Jesus—the one who would minister particularly among the poor, the humble and the unknown.

The birth of John the Baptist (1:57-80)

It seems Elizabeth's family only knew of her experiences after John was born. She used the family gathering as an opportunity to speak of the goodness of God. Her neighbours and relatives 'heard how the Lord had shown great mercy to her' and 'rejoiced with her' (v. 58). To rejoice publicly in the goodness of God is honouring to him, and others may catch the flame and rejoice also.

John was circumcised according to Jewish law on the eighth day and thus the time had come to name him. Many expected him to be called 'Zacharias', after his father, but, resisting family pressure and social custom, Zacharias wrote down 'his name is John', as the angel had told him (v. 13). Not only was this choice a break with convention, but it was also symbolic of John's unique life, for he, too, had to swim against the current.

When Zacharias had fulfilled his duty, he could speak again. Instead of voicing frustration or anger at the God who had silenced him, 'he spoke, *praising God*' (v. 64). It is a great mercy from God when we are able to see God's hand in our trials and to praise him when they are over.

We may wonder how it was that John could be a man of the desert, resisting the customs and values around him, and warning all men from Roman soldiers to Herod himself. Using an expression found several times in the Old Testament, Luke tells us, 'the hand of the Lord was with him' (v. 66).

Zacharias, like his wife Elizabeth, was filled with the Holy Spirit. As this occurred, he prophesied concerning the days of the Messiah, whom he called, the 'horn of salvation' (v. 69). A horn symbolizes strength. The Lord Jesus would be the strong deliverer and liberator. Yet once the people are free, Zacharias does not speak of them selfishly pursuing their own pleasures but instead (vv. 74, 75) says that they will use their freedom to serve God without fear, 'in holiness and righteousness before him all the days of our life'.

Zacharias finally turns to the little child he had desired for so long. He says John will be called 'the prophet of the highest' (v. 76). He will prepare the way for Jesus the Messiah. John was to plough the soil that Christ would sow.

Thus John the Baptist's ministry is foretold. The chapter ends with John growing up and becoming 'strong in spirit'. He starts to lead a solitary, desert life as a young man, 'till the day of his manifestation to Israel'.

FOR FURTHER STUDY

1. Names are important in the Bible. How do we know that these people had personalities in keeping with their names? Naomi (see Ruth 1:20, 21), Nabal (see 1 Sam. 25:25); consider also Miriam, Jezebel and Onesimus.
2. 'The hand of the Lord' (v. 66). Look up this expression in Ezra 7:6, 9, 28; 8:18, 22, 31 and Nehemiah 2:8, 18, etc. What difference did it make when the hand of the Lord was with them?
3. Consider how being filled with the Holy Spirit is often accompanied by speaking out. See Luke1:41, 42 and 67, 68; also Acts 2:4; 4:8, 31. It seems he equips God's people to speak boldly and eloquently. See how he is also associated with joy (Acts 13:52).
4. Is it important for us to be aware of our sins before we are saved (Luke 1:77)?

TO THINK ABOUT AND DISCUSS

1. Read Luke 1:48. Since so many seem to bow down to Mary, are we in danger of over-reacting to this and despising her?
2. Elizabeth told 'neighbours and relatives' of God's blessings (v. 58). How can God's blessings be used as an opportunity for witness to others?
3. See Luke 1:59-63. Think of examples of how believers today resist social and family pressure.
4. Do we use the freedom we have to serve God in the way outlined in Luke 1:74, 75?
5. What would have been different about the ministry of Jesus if there had been no John the Baptist?

2 Luke Chapter 2

The Bible never wastes words and, in just seven verses, Luke tells us a great deal. Familiarity with the account of the birth of Jesus can make us 'switch off' as we read. Yet the events as told by Luke reveal that despite the suffering inflicted by the Romans upon the Jews, and the hardships endured by Mary and Joseph, God's unseen hand was at work in it all.

The birth of Jesus (2:1-7)

The circumstances of our Lord's birth are well known; a Roman census for tax purposes was commanded. God directed even the moment when Roman greed would lead to this decree. Jesus was to be born in Bethlehem, thus fulfilling Old Testament prophecy (Micah 5:2).

After a long journey of some seventy-five miles undertaken by Mary, heavily pregnant, she and Joseph arrived at Bethlehem. The inn (which in biblical times would have had an open-plan sleeping area) was full, and therefore

Mary and Joseph had to go to what seems to have been a stable (because of the reference to a 'manger'), possibly constructed from a natural cave.

It may have seemed strange to the couple to find the inn closed to them in this way. Angels had spoken of the glorious nature of their child, yet there was no open home in which he could be born. The Lord Jesus had 'nowhere to lay his head' during his ministry (Luke 9:58) and so it was at his birth. Midwives emphasize good hygiene whenever a woman gives birth, yet in this account we see that God made sure that Mary and her baby were kept safe, despite unhygienic conditions around them in the stable. When God blesses and protects, we need not fear.

Light in obscurity (2:8-20)

Ordinary shepherds were to be the first to see Jesus. The wise men in Matthew 2:1-12 saw the Saviour in a 'house' (Matt. 2:11), which may well have been where the family moved to shortly after the birth. A group of shepherds would become the first people outside of Jesus' family to know of his arrival (Luke 2:8-20).

We often think in our society that to have an impact we must harness the forces of earthly power. If only Christians controlled TV! If only Christians ruled the nations! Yet God's way is often very different. The Gospel of Luke teaches us that God can take obscure and poor people and use them to transform the world.

How joyfully the angel, and later the 'multitude of the heavenly host', celebrate the birth of Christ! Jesus, the one who would usher in the 'glad tidings' of the gospel, was born.

It was only fitting for the skies to ring out:

'Glory to God in the highest,
And on earth peace,
goodwill toward men!' (v. 14)

The shepherds rushed to see the infant Christ, and then made known what they had heard concerning the child. Shepherds became the first New Testament evangelists!

FOR FURTHER STUDY

1. Bethlehem was the birthplace of King David. In his youth, he cared for sheep in that area. Look up 1 Samuel 17:34-37.
2. Ordinary shepherds were the first visitors to see the Lord in a manger. In the Acts of the Apostles, we find that disciples of Jesus were uneducated, ordinary men (Acts 4:13).
3. Compare the spontaneous proclamation of the shepherds (2:17, 18) with the joy 'Legion' had when healed by the Lord (Luke 8:39).

TO THINK ABOUT AND DISCUSS

1. Caesar Augustus made a proclamation at just the right time. How far does God direct the thoughts and actions of all leaders (see Prov. 21:1)?
2. Many think that God would like to have the most spectacular publicity, in order to achieve a world-following at any cost. If that were so, then Caesar himself in Rome might have been told in a dream of the birth of Christ. Instead the news is revealed to shepherds. Think how often it is that God exalts those of low birth, and sends the rich away empty (1:52, 53). What modern examples of this principle can you think of?
3. Jesus had a room remarkably supplied for the Passover meal with his disciples (Luke 22:7-13). Why, therefore, was there no such room supplied for Mary and Joseph to stay in?

4. Why, in your opinion, does Luke tell us about the shepherds but not the visit of the wise men, the Magi?

The child presented to God (2:21-40)

The infant Messiah is given a name. We may ask, 'What's in a name?' but in the Bible names are very important. 'Jesus' was literally 'Yeshua', meaning, 'Saviour' (see Matt. 1:21).

Verse 24 indicates to us the financial circumstances of Mary and Joseph. Mary's forty-day purification was over.[1] The couple, according to the Law of Moses, prepared an offering of two turtledoves or young pigeons to God. This offering was permitted for those who were too poor to afford a lamb as the offering (see Lev. 12:8). We see, therefore, just how poor Mary and Joseph were.

The verses which follow tell of two elderly people who were faithful and zealous in the service of God, and who walked closely with him. Careful reading of the opening four chapters of this Gospel shows that the blessings brought by Jesus were for people of every age, race and background.

Simeon: a man ready to die (2:25-35)

Simeon was told by God that 'he would not see death before he had seen the Lord's Christ'. This man was guided by the Holy Spirit to enter the Temple at just the right moment. He took the child in his arms and said words that reach us today with the same depth and power they must have had when first uttered:

> Lord, now lettest thou thy servant depart in peace,
> according to thy word:

for mine eyes have seen
thy salvation. (AV)

Here is an old man who now felt ready to die. He had not seen a miracle performed by Jesus, nor had he heard a word of his matchless teaching. There was nothing remarkable in either the parents or the child to mark Jesus out visibly; yet Simeon felt ready to die, for he had seen the Messiah. Simeon says, 'Mine eyes have seen *thy salvation*'. Here was not only the Saviour, but he represented, even as an infant, salvation itself. Wrapped up in the life of this child was all the hope there could ever be in this world of sadness and pain.

Anna the prophetess (2:36-40)

Anna was a woman with great passion for God. She was a widow, eighty-four years old. Her entire life was devoted to prayer and fasting night and day. She belonged to the tribe of Asher, one of the northern ten tribes of Israel which were all but lost after captivity in Babylon some 500 years before. She lived in absolute devotion to God, and the Lord blessed her with a sight of the infant Messiah, Jesus. She told everyone who looked for redemption in Jerusalem that their Deliverer had come, and she had seen him.

Mary and Joseph eventually returned to Nazareth. There Jesus 'grew and became strong in spirit, filled with wisdom; and the grace of God was upon him' (v. 40). The Bible teaches that he is fully God and fully man. As God, he knew all things; but as a human being his knowledge had to increase over time (see notes on Luke 2:47).

Jesus amazes the teachers (2:41-52)

Jesus was now twelve years old. Nothing is told us in any of the Gospels of his character and work from his infancy until the age of thirty, except here. This incident is recorded to teach us about the developing ministry and wisdom of the Lord in his youth.

The Passover was a feast officially lasting eight days. Mary, Joseph and other family members, including probably our Lord's four half-brothers and half-sisters (see Matt. 13:55, 56) had attended Jerusalem for Passover. The book of Exodus teaches that all the males of Israel were expected at Jerusalem three times a year for Passover, the Feast of Firstfruits and the Feast of Ingathering at harvest (Exod. 34:22,23).

This would have been costly. For Joseph, probably a self-employed carpenter, it was not easy to abandon his trade. Also, leaving homes and livestock unattended for several days would have been hard. Yet God promised protection of their property (Exod. 34:23, 24). We are made aware of Mary's spiritual priorities in that she wished to worship God in Jerusalem, and not stay behind.

'When they had finished the days' (v. 43), that is, when the feast was over, Mary, Joseph and the extended family began to travel back to Nazareth. They travelled for one day, and then could not find Jesus. Three days of weary searching among crowds of pilgrims in Jerusalem finally led them to him.

What had the Son of God been doing? The religious leaders had been listening carefully to the young man, and all those who heard him were 'astonished at his understanding and answers' (v. 47). Physically the Lord grew naturally, at the same rate as his peers. His vocabulary was probably consistent with his age as he grew. We are not told, for instance, that he preached to the shepherds as a newborn infant! Yet he was different from any other young pilgrim to Jerusalem. His understanding was way beyond his years, for here was the Son of God growing to maturity.

When he asked his parents, 'Why did you seek me?' he seemed concerned that, knowing about the great task he was to perform, their search had not taken them immediately to the Temple. This vast area of courts and terraces was built on a platform three quarters of a mile in circumference.[2] The Temple area not only housed the Holy Place itself, but enclosed a vast area where people sought the face of God, worshipped him and discussed spiritual things. 'Did you not know that I must be about my Father's business?' (v. 49). Our Lord's entire life was centred upon the will of his Father (see Ps. 40:7, 8 and John 4:34).

Mary and Joseph were ordinary people who did not always grasp the full meaning of spiritual truth. It is all the more remarkable that our Lord, in obedience to the fifth commandment, was able to recognize their authority as parents, and be 'subject to them'.

They did not understand his words (v. 50). Mary and Joseph were ordinary people who did not always grasp the full meaning of spiritual truth. It is all the more remarkable that our Lord, in obedience to the fifth commandment, was able to recognize their authority as parents, and be 'subject to them' (v. 51). He acknowledged their God-given rights over him, however poor their understanding may at times have seemed to him.

Mary and Joseph had spoken with an angel and seen the miracle of Jesus' birth, yet still their understanding of Christ's mission was limited. No matter how many encounters with the spiritual realm we may have had, we still have to pray daily for discernment to grasp and to obey the will of God.

FOR FURTHER STUDY

1. What does Colossians 2:3 teach us about the wisdom of Christ?

2. See Luke 2:52. The Lord Jesus grew in wisdom, stature and favour. Consider and compare what is said about the prophet Samuel as he grew up (1 Sam. 2:21, 26 and 3:19).

3. How should we understand the relationship Jesus had with his heavenly Father in John 4:34?

4. It must at times have been very hard for the Lord of glory to submit to Mary and Joseph as parents, yet he did so. How important is it for us to honour our parents throughout life? (See Exod. 20:12; Judg. 14:16 and Prov. 1:8, 9.)

TO THINK ABOUT AND DISCUSS

1. God protected his people's possessions when they visited Jerusalem, so that they did not need to worry about property being stolen, or misused (Exod. 34:23, 24). How important to God is it for us to worship him without fretting or distraction?

2. Mary and Joseph left the carpentry shop and sought to worship God. How far does the way we spend our time reflect our spiritual priorities?

3. Do we underestimate the spiritual insight of young people?

4. Luke 2:43-46 shows that Mary and Joseph had travelled without being conscious of the absence of Jesus. What does this teach us about the need to be aware of Christ's presence or absence in our daily lives?

5. See erse. 50. Mary and Joseph were not always able to understand what they were told. Why are we so slow to believe and grasp the word of God? (Note the difficulty our Lord's disciples had—Luke 9:45 and 18:34.)

3 Luke
Chapter 3

In the opening verses of this chapter, the precision of Luke's approach is apparent. Matthew writes simply, 'In those days John the Baptist came preaching in the wilderness of Judea…' (Matt. 3:1). Luke, however, gives us a cross-reference to the exact time when John began his ministry.

Luke's precision (3:1-6) (see table on page 220)

John began preaching between AD 26 and AD 33. According to Josephus, Annas was acting High Priest in AD 26. Many believe therefore that our Lord's ministry began in the late 20s AD.

John had already spent years in the wilderness (see Luke 1:80). Now, finally, 'the word of God' came to him. His task was to prepare the way for the Messiah.

In order to reach the lost, we often desire to use glossy brochures and professionally produced presentations given by men in clean, expensive suits. Yet John the Baptist cuts through all this. He appears clothed in camel's hair, with a leather belt (see Mark 1:6), rather like a citizen of another world. He neither aspires to affluence nor tries to impress with fine clothes. Surely we can learn from John's rugged and forthright purity.

John's task was not easy, as Isaiah tells us (Isa. 40:3-5). His voice had to cry out in the heat and barrenness of the desert. The obstacles in the path of the Messiah were many: valleys to be filled, mountains to be flattened, crooked places to be straightened, and all flesh made to see. He was paving the way for the Lord Jesus.

John's baptism was a 'baptism of repentance' (v. 3). The Jews were familiar with ceremonial washings and times of 'bathing in water' anytime they became unclean (see Lev. 15:5-8, 11, 13, 16, 18, 22, 27). However, John's baptism was a sign, not as yet of faith, but of sorrow for sin; a symbol of cleansing from all that is wrong.

John's powerful preaching (3:7-20)

John was outspoken and direct. He warned the people that they were a 'brood of vipers' (v. 7), that is, they posed a genuine danger to others; for they appeared sincere and religious, yet were full of poison. John wanted to see believers bearing fruits 'worthy of repentance' (vv. 8ff), that is, living lives which pleased God. Today we have become very superficial, believing repentance to be nothing more than a quiet apology to God. Scripturally, it involves a total change of mindset, life and direction.

John tells the multitude to bear fruit, and not to rely on their Jewish inheritance or the fact of their descent from godly Abraham. Fruitless trees will be cut down, however noble their root!

John instructs the people to share even fifty per cent of what they have, giving away their surplus goods (v. 11). How different was John's life and message from the materialism so dear to our hearts.

It must by now have been clear to the people that, however dramatic and far-reaching John's ministry seemed to be, the ministry of Christ would be far greater. John baptized with water, Christ with the Holy Spirit and fire.

Next, tax collectors come to him. Theirs was a hated occupation, not only since the money collected paid for the Romans to continue their oppression of Israel, but tax collectors themselves often took more than their due. The name 'tax collector' was synonymous with *unbeliever*, even from our Lord's perspective (Matt. 18:17). John tells the tax collectors to take no more than is appointed to them. He desired the good of all, however despised they might be, telling soldiers not to abuse their power. Intimidation, false accusation and covetousness are attacked in one statement (v. 14).

In the verses that follow, the crowd is naturally curious about the identity of John. Is he the Christ, that is, the Messiah or anointed one, promised so long before? John answers plainly that he is not the Christ. Indeed, he felt unworthy even to loose his sandal strap (v. 16).

John always recognized the temporary nature of his own ministry; his job was to prepare the way for his Lord. It must by now have been clear to the people that, however dramatic and far-reaching John's ministry seemed to be, the ministry of Christ would be far greater. John baptized with water, Christ with the Holy Spirit and fire. John spoke of trees cut down; Jesus will burn the chaff with 'unquenchable fire' (Luke 3:15-17).

John's imprisonment (3:19, 20)

Although John was present at the baptism of Jesus, Luke tells of his imprisonment here. In organizing the material for the Gospel, Luke wanted to convey that John's clear and decisive testimony extended beyond tax collectors and soldiers to Herod himself.

John was fair-minded and not one to consider his own safety. Nor did he speak generally, with such vagueness as never to give offence. He clearly denounced Herod's adultery, in taking his brother's wife.[3]

John's long imprisonment surprises us. We may ask, 'Why did God allow such a great man to be silenced?' Yet it must be remembered that God has good reasons, which are clear to him. Herod listened to John while he was in prison (Mark 6:16-20). In the darkness of a prison cell, John was able to warn and to teach this powerful ruler. Later, in Luke 9:9, Herod wanted to see Jesus and hear him also.

Jesus baptized (3:21, 22)

Baptism is a symbol of death and new life. Romans 6:4 reveals that baptism symbolizes death to self, and the beginning of a new life in the spirit. When people are baptized, it is to show that they belong to the Lord and seek to 'walk in newness of life' (Rom. 6:4). John was surprised that a rite which expressed repentance should be observed by one who was without sin. Yet the Lord Jesus wanted to show that there is no area of obedience which he was not willing to undergo first.

It was not only John's voice, crying in the wilderness, that ushered in the ministry of God's Son. The voice of God himself declared the unique identity of the person who was baptized: 'You are my beloved son; in you I am well pleased.'

The family tree (3:23-38)

This 'genealogy' is very important, since it shows our Lord's descent through Joseph, his stepfather, back to David. Remarkably, it stretches further back, even to Judah and on to the patriarchs, ending with Adam. This genealogy, written by a man with such respect for authenticity and detail as Luke, emphasizes the reliability of the Bible. If Jesus and Joseph the carpenter are historical figures, then why not Abraham, Noah and Adam also?

Luke takes us back as far as the first man, whereas the list in Matthew 1 extends only as far as Abraham. This is partly because Matthew wanted to show us that there is a symmetry to Bible history comprising periods of fourteen generations (see Matt. 1:17). Also, he wanted to emphasize our Lord's descent from Abraham, the father of the Jewish people, and David, their greatest king (see Matt. 1:1).

In Luke's account, Adam is called 'the son of God' because he is the first man created by him, and the first to be made in his image. Christ is the Son of God not by creation, but because he shares in the divinity of the Father, and has done so for all eternity (John 17:5).

The Lord Jesus descends from the tribe of Judah. The writer to the Hebrews points out that Judah was not a tribe of priests (Heb. 7:14), so that we can see that the Lord does not have an *inherited* right to priesthood, but an eternal one (Heb. 7:16).

FOR FURTHER STUDY

1. Mark 1:6 gives us a description of John. How does his appearance tie in with his message?
2. Consider Luke 3:16 in the light of Acts 2:2-4.
3. In the Bible, the Holy Spirit is compared to the elements, water, fire and the wind. Can you recall where?
4. From Mark 16:16, how important is baptism?
5. John called upon the people to reveal true repentance by changed lives. How far is this emphasized in Ephesians 4:28-32 and James 2:14-18?
6. The Lord Jesus was baptized in order to 'fulfil all righteousness' (Matt. 3:15). His followers are also expected to be baptized. In what other ways did Christ do first that which he now demands of us?

TO THINK ABOUT AND DISCUSS

1. Considering John the Baptist, how important is the way we dress when we are trying to reach others for Christ?
2. Do we stand out from the materialism and ambition of the world in our desires and way of life?
3. Looking at 3:5, did John face greater spiritual obstacles ('valleys', 'mountains' and 'crooked places') than we have today?

4. Why did so many come to hear John (v. 7), when his message was one of repentance, and must have sounded negative?

5. John was not content to baptize; he wanted to see changed lives. Do our lives today show that we really understand 'repentance'?

6. We all have surplus goods; how can we apply Luke 3:11 today?

7. Luke 3:14. Should all people be content with their wages?

8. Luke 3:19. Do Christians today have the right to denounce the specific sins of their rulers?

9. 'Luke's genealogy reads as authentic history. Indeed to prove the truth of the Old Testament, you have only to believe the New Testament.' Discuss this statement.

4 Luke Chapter 4

This chapter begins with the temptation of Jesus. Following his baptism, the Lord undertakes a forty-day fast. At the end of this period, Satan tempts him. Nowhere since the book of Job have we seen so clearly the power and deceit of Satan.

Satan's strategy (4:1-13)

Satan attacks us most viciously after a time of blessing. In our Lord's case, it was immediately after his baptism, and following a time of deep communion with his Father.

Satan wanted Jesus to question his relationship with his Father: 'If you are the Son of God' (v. 3). In a similar way, he tries to make believers question their salvation.

Satan preys upon one's current area of weakness. In our Lord's case the first temptation related to his hunger after such a long fast.

Satan has great power over the kingdoms of the world (vv. 5, 6). He claims that their authority and glory belong to him. It is noteworthy that the Lord resists him without questioning the fact of his earthly power.

Satan knows Scripture, and twists it to his advantage. Here he deliberately quotes, out of context, the promise contained in Psalm 91:10, 11.

The Saviour does not mock the devil, but answers his enticements with Scripture. Peter warns us that the devil is an adversary as fierce as a roaring lion (1 Peter 5:8). The apostle Paul tells us we need armour to face him (Eph. 6:11). Among the items of this armour listed by Paul is the 'sword of the Spirit, which is the word of God' (Eph. 6:17). The Lord Jesus is, of course, totally familiar with the word of God, and used it to resist the devil. Satan is a formidable foe, but his strategies can be thwarted. Christ's example teaches us that Satan's lies and temptations can be overcome by carefully opposing him with Scripture.

FOR FURTHER STUDY

1. Luke 4:2. Forty-day fasts were undertaken by Moses in Mount Sinai (Exod. 34:27, 28) and Elijah as he approached the same mountain (1 Kings 19:7, 8). What were the reasons for such a fast?

2. The book of Deuteronomy had to be written out by kings, and be read all the days of their lives (see Deut. 17:18-20). Is this why the Lord Jesus, who is King of kings, used Deuteronomy to refute the devil?

3. Luke 4:12. How can we differentiate between trusting God, which is a virtue, and tempting God, which is a vice?

4. Satan departed until 'an opportune time' (v. 13). What situations and times are particularly 'opportune' for his temptation (see Gen. 3:1-6)?

5. Two of the Gospels tell us that angels ministered to the Lord after his temptations (Matt. 4:11, Mark 1:13). Read also of the comfort given to the Saviour by angels in the Garden of Gethsemane (Luke 22:43). How do they help believers today?

TO THINK ABOUT AND DISCUSS

1. Why, when Christ was 'filled with the Holy Spirit' and 'led by the Spirit' (Luke 4:1), did he find himself tempted by the devil in the wilderness?
2. Are our most spiritually blessed times always followed by temptation and opposition from the devil?
3. The Son of God fasted, and assumed his followers would fast (Matt. 6:16). Why is this practice so neglected today? What are the benefits of fasting?
4. What scriptures, from anywhere in the Bible, could you use to oppose Satan's temptations in these areas: stealing; lying; sexual temptation; drunkenness?
5. Read Luke 4:5, 6. How far does the power of the devil extend in this world? (See 2 Cor. 4:4).

Jesus hated in his home town (4:14-30)

In Galilee, Jesus 'taught in their synagogues, being glorified by all' (v. 15). Mark tells us that the Saviour preached repentance at this time (Mark 1:15). During this period, he performed his first miracle of turning water into wine (John 2:1-11). However, storms gathered when he returned to his hometown of Nazareth.

Nazareth was situated in Galilee, an area in which God's people were surrounded by Gentiles. Jews in Jerusalem regarded themselves as somewhat superior to those who lived in Galilee. Their willingness to live outside of the centre of Judaism, Jerusalem, meant they were to some degree isolated. It was his rustic Galilean accent which gave Peter away as a disciple of Jesus of Nazareth (see Matt. 26:69, 73).

Although born in Bethlehem, it was in Nazareth of Galilee

that Christ grew up. He would become known as 'Jesus of Nazareth'. This town is not even mentioned in the Old Testament and was regarded with especial contempt (John 1:46), perhaps for its dirty streets and poverty, or the aggression of its residents. Several instances in the Gospels suggest the people of Nazareth were scathing and fiery. Satan had left the Lord 'until an opportune time' (v. 13). Such a time had now come. He had sought to tempt Jesus to leap from the pinnacle of the temple. It is as if he raises a crowd to throw him to his death in Nazareth.

Our Lord travelled to his hometown and entered the synagogue. There he was handed the book of Isaiah and, as in the opening verses of this chapter, his wonderful familiarity with Scripture became evident. He found the place where it speaks of the glory of the Messiah's work (Isa. 61) and read it out. Without any miracle or sign to prove his identity, the Lord closed the scroll and sat down. At this stage, it seemed all were amazed at him. How his words must have astonished all who heard them: 'Today this Scripture is fulfilled in your hearing' (v. 21).

Jesus revealed that he would not be well received among his own people, but, like the prophets of old, he would be accepted by Gentiles. Elijah was sent to the gentile widow of Zarephath, to keep her from starvation, and Elisha to pagan Naaman, to bring healing from leprosy.

Jesus revealed that he would not be well received among

his own people, but, like the prophets of old, he would be accepted by Gentiles. Elijah was sent to the gentile widow of Zarephath, to keep her from starvation, and Elisha to pagan Naaman, to bring healing from leprosy.

It seems it was this emphasis which angered the crowd. 'So all those in the synagogue, when they heard these things, were filled with wrath' (v. 28). In their mad rage, and without any respect for a proper trial, they tried to hurl the Lord from the brow of a cliff upon which the city was built.

Amazingly (and this would not be the last time) Jesus passed through the hostile crowd and 'went his way'.

FOR FURTHER STUDY

1. 'Filled with the Holy Spirit', 'led by the Spirit', 'returned in the power of the Spirit', 'the Spirit of the LORD is upon me' (Luke 4:1,14,18). Consider these words in the light of John 3:34.
2. The age of the Messiah was seen in the Old Testament as a time of great joy. How would the expressions in Isaiah 61:1, 2 have been understood by those who first heard them? How do we apply them today?
3. Consider Luke 4:30 alongside John 7:29, 30, 44; 8:39 and John 10:59. What were the circumstances in which the Saviour passed through hostile crowds? What does this tell us about the voluntary nature of his death on the cross?

TO THINK ABOUT AND DISCUSS

1. Read Luke 4:18. During his ministry, Christ stressed that the good news, the 'gospel', is for the poor (see also Luke 7:22). Why does he say this?
2. How often has your daily Bible reading been exactly relevant for that day? Can you

give examples?

3. See Luke 4:16. In New Testament times, synagogues allowed visitors to speak to the whole gathering (Acts 13:14, 15). Would it be a good thing for churches to allow this today? Consider points both 'for' and 'against' this idea.

4. 'No prophet is accepted in his own country' (v. 24). Are evangelists and preachers generally more useful in ministry outside the locality in which they grew up?

The healing ministry of Jesus begins (4:31-44)

To some it is a puzzle as to why so much of the Gospel narrative is devoted to healing. They grow weary of the lists of people relieved of pain and infirmity. Yet, if you have ever had a serious illness, the sweetness and beauty of our Lord's healing ministry comes to life. We rejoice in the great relief and joy given to so many people. Additionally, our Lord's healing ministry gave tangible evidence of his identity as the Son of God.

Jesus went to Capernaum, on the Sea of Galilee (see map on page 9). So frequent were his visits to this seaside town, that it was called 'his own city' (Matt. 9:1).

In the synagogue, a man possessed by a demon cried out. In Luke 4:34, 41, demons recognized the identity of Jesus as the 'Holy One of God', 'the Christ, the Son of God'. How different *recognition* of him is from *faith* in him! James tells us that even demons believe and tremble before God (James 2:19).

Jesus rebuked the demons because his time for public recognition had not yet come. Later he would also tell the people he healed to say nothing about him (Luke 5:14, 8:56, 9:20, 21 etc). The demon in verse 34 recognized Jesus as his judge, the one who would one day 'destroy'. He will eternally condemn those who reject him. The Lord rebuked the demon, who left the man, doing him no harm (v. 35b).

The Saviour healed Simon's mother-in-law (vv. 38, 39). The three synoptic Gospels all record this healing. Clearly we are meant to see that following Jesus was costly, because we learn that Simon Peter had a wife and extended family. We have not yet read in this Gospel of his contact with Simon Peter himself. It seems that Christ had made friends with most of his disciples before the moment when he officially called them (see Luke 6:13-16). Once Simon's mother-in-law was well, she immediately served others. How important it is for those who recover from sickness to use their strength to minister to other people!

Jesus told the people, as he taught and healed, that he had to minister to others also (vv. 42, 43). He had been sent to preach far and wide throughout Israel, not just to the communities in Galilee.

FOR FURTHER STUDY

1. See Luke 4:36. When Jesus rebuked a demon, the people recognized that his power was manifested in his words. How is this borne out in Revelation 1:16? Consider also Ecclesiastes 8:4.
2. Some believe demon possession in biblical times was merely a form of epilepsy. How does a careful study of the list in Matthew 4:24 disprove this?
3. Christ silenced demons, even as they uttered the truth about him (Luke 4:34, 41 and 8:28). For what reason did Paul and Silas do this in Philippi (Acts 16:16-18)?
4. Luke 4:40. The Messiah healed 'every one' who came to him. What is the impact of this form of expression, as we compare it with Acts 5:16?

TO THINK ABOUT AND DISCUSS

1. How far is physical illness a hindrance to our spiritual life?

2. Refer to Luke 4:34. Demons recognized the identity of Christ as the Holy One. Are people worse than demons when they do not?

3. Does demon possession occur today? Provide a reason or reasons for your answer. How far would people who are demon-possessed still be accountable for their actions in the sight of God?

5 Luke Chapter 5

Such was the hunger for the word of God that the people, listening to Jesus, 'pressed about him' (v. 1), and he had to teach them from a boat!

The miraculous catch of fish (5:1-11)

The Lord then instructed Simon ('Peter') to 'launch out into the deep and let down your nets for a catch' (v. 4). This may have seemed foolish to the fisherman, since the best time for catching fish—the night—had passed and there were no fish to show for it. Yet Simon submitted: 'Nevertheless at your word…' (v. 5). Mary had learnt this lesson a few days before when she said to servants at a wedding in Cana, 'Whatever he says to you, do it' (John 2:5). However uncomfortable the commands of Christ may sound, let those who claim to follow him be swift to obey his voice.

The great catch that followed nearly ruined a net and almost sank two ships! Simon's reaction to this astounding miracle seems strange. He fell down and said, 'Depart from me, for I am a sinful man, O Lord!' (v. 8). There is something totally overwhelming about the moment when a sinner comes face to face with the kindness and power of the Lord. Everyone who witnessed this miracle was astonished. The Lord called James, John and Simon to follow him: 'Do not be afraid. From now on you will catch men' (v. 10). With that, they brought their boats to shore, 'forsook all and followed him'. In just a few words, Luke describes what for some people seems unthinkable—to leave those closest to us and live with no certain means of sustenance and support.

A great deal of fuss is made today about the importance of 'claiming' healing as a right. Many sick people are told that it is their own lack of confidence to demand healing from God which keeps them unwell. Yet here we see a leper asking with complete submission to the will of Christ.

The submissive leper (5:12-16)

A great deal of fuss is made today about the importance of 'claiming' healing as a right. Many sick people are told that it is their own lack of confidence to demand healing from God which keeps them unwell. Yet here we see a leper asking with complete submission to the will of Christ. He stands as a perpetual rebuke to those who would try to wrench blessings from the hands of God.

He was 'full of leprosy' (v. 12). This dreaded skin disease would have rendered him an outcast. He had to live separately from the rest of his family. In all, his was a most miserable, painful and humiliating life. Yet the leper approached the Lord with an attitude of submission. Matthew records that his prostration was an act of worship (Matt. 8:2). He 'fell on his face and implored him, saying, "Lord, if you are willing, you can make me clean"' (v. 12). Too often we are afraid to commit our situation to the will of the Lord and this betrays mistrust of him. Yet the leper trusted the kindness and mercy of the Lord enough to submit to his will.

The Lord answered, 'I am willing; be cleansed' (v. 13). Immediately the leprosy left the man. Next he instructed him to go through the eight-day ritual cleansing commanded by the Law of Moses (Lev. 14—see also Luke 17:14).

As multitudes came to be healed (v. 15), the time came for the Son of God to withdraw and be once more alone with his Father.

FOR FURTHER STUDY

1. Read Luke 5:4. Christ told the disciples to 'let down your nets'. In Cana he said, fill six pots with water (John 2:7); he told a blind man to wash in the pool of Siloam (John 9:11). These commands may have seemed strange or even absurd to those who first heard them. Yet in each case, they revealed the power of the Lord, and brought blessing. Are we the best judges of which commands of Christ are 'practical' and which are not?
2. Read Leviticus 13:45, 46. Lepers were kept separate from the wider community. This was very harsh for the individual, but necessary for the protection of the community. What moral principles may be enshrined here?
3. See Luke 5:12. Have we learnt to delight in the will of God for our lives? Are we willing to say, as the Lord's prayer teaches us, 'Thy will be done…' (Matt. 6:10, AV)? Our Lord himself said, 'I delight to do your will, O my God' (Ps. 40:8). Which areas of

submission do we find easiest, and which most difficult?

4. Read Luke 5:14-16. Why did Jesus try to limit the publicity he was experiencing?

5. During the ritual cleansing of a leper (v. 14), one bird is killed and another bird set free (Lev. 14:4-7). What is here taught concerning the atonement of Christ?

TO THINK ABOUT AND DISCUSS

1. What created such hunger in the people that they had to hear the word of God?

2. Jesus taught sitting down (Luke 5:3). Is posture important in preaching?

3. The fishermen were told to go back after a night of toil and to fish again. Does the Lord expect a greater output of zeal and energy in obeying him than we imagine?

4. Peter felt his own sinfulness when confronted with the Lord's power and kindness (v. 8). How far does Romans 2:3, 4 teach us to expect this?

5. Luke 5:10. Evangelism is compared to fishing. What lessons can we draw from this metaphor? (Consider the need for patience, the use of bait, etc.)

6. Read Luke 5:12 and suggest why it might be offensive to God to claim healing as a right.

Healing and conflict (5:17-39)

Christ often spoke to religious leaders. The Pharisees (see endnote 9) and teachers of the law had travelled far and wide to hear him. As they gathered to hear Jesus, 'the power of the Lord was present to heal them' (v. 17). Then, strangely, a paralysed man was let down through the roof tiling by his friends. Such was the determination of his friends, they resorted to this method of gaining the Lord's attention.

Jesus pronounced the man forgiven—the most important blessing he could give. Yet forgiveness has an *invisible* effect.

The people were angry, since no one has the right to forgive sins but God alone. No prophet or religious leader in the Old Testament had ever claimed such authority. Yet Jesus does so, for he is God.

Next, Christ astounded the crowd as they witnessed the *visible* transformation of the man. He told the man to rise, and healed him. It is clear from Luke 5:24 that the healing was designed to give evidence of the man's forgiveness. He arose, took up his mat and went home, 'glorifying God'. The reaction was electrifying (v. 26). No one had seen the power of God at work in this way before.

In this chapter, Luke introduces us to some of our Lord's friends and foes then continues by describing the calling of Levi, otherwise known as Matthew (Luke 5:27-39). Jesus found Levi sitting down to receive money. Tax collectors were despised for reasons considered in the notes on Luke 3:12, 13.

Levi was called to follow Jesus, and left everything. That very day he arranged a feast for his tax collector friends. What a testimony it is when those who knew us before our encounter with Christ are invited to dinner, and see the difference!

The scribes and the Pharisees were also present, and used the otherwise happy event to criticize Jesus. They commented on his disciples' willingness to eat and drink with tax collectors and sinners. His reply was characteristic (Luke 5:31, 32). Just as earlier in the chapter the Saviour healed the leper who was an outcast because of his sickness, so here he sought to bring the good news of salvation to those who were morally 'sick'. In his compassion, the Lord viewed their crimes as a sickness requiring healing.

As the meal was in progress and everyone was enjoying the food, the Lord's ministry came under attack again. This time he was criticized for having disciples who ate heartily, and drank wine as others! What little time was Jesus permitted even for relaxation and the enjoyment of a meal.

Christ responded by saying that he, as the bridegroom, was physically present with his people. Yet one day he would leave, and then they would fast. He proceeded by describing the entire renewal required by members of his kingdom. New wine requires new wineskins; otherwise the process of fermentation will cause the skin to break. Those who baulked at his teaching were like old wineskins that refused anything they could not understand. Jesus made the point that most prefer the old wine, not the new glorious wine of his kingdom.

FOR FURTHER STUDY

1. Read Matthew 23 where Pharisees and scribes are fiercely rebuked by the Lord. To whom might we apply these words today?
2. See Luke 5:20, 21. In Psalm 130:3, 4 we learn that forgiveness belongs to God alone. Thus, by declaring that a man's sins were forgiven, our Lord demonstrated his divinity. What else do we learn from Psalm 130:3, 4?
3. To what extent was Christ speaking with irony when he said there are some who 'have no need of a physician' (Luke 5:31)?
4. Consider Luke 5:30-32. Should we follow our Lord's example and mix with the ungodly, if we can do them good? See 1 Peter 1:21, 22.

TO THINK ABOUT AND DISCUSS

1. Does Luke 5:17b suggest that there are certain times when God's power to heal is particularly known? Do such times occur today?
2. The paralysed man had friends who would stop at nothing to see him well again (vv. 18-20). How determined and persevering should we be in prayer for a friend or relative to be healed?
3. List the three main reactions to our Lord's healing (Luke 5:26). Can you explain the reason for each one?
4. How different would that day have been if the Lord had forgiven the paralysed man, but left him still sick?
5. Matthew threw a feast for tax collectors in his own house (v. 29). Jesus also allowed his followers to join him at the dinner and influence sinners for good. What should be our ground rules for socializing with the ungodly?
6. To what extent can sin be compared to sickness (vv. 31, 32)? What are the implications for our compassion toward the lost?

6 Luke Chapter 6

Throughout history, the gift of the Sabbath day has been one of the greatest benefits to the human race. Through it, God our Creator granted to us a day of refreshment for our bodies and food for our souls.

The Sabbath understood (6:1-11)

The religious leaders in New Testament times had added many man-made restrictions to the wholesome teaching of God. The whole point of the day as a benefit for people and a day to worship God was choked by such regulations.

One Sabbath day, Christ and his disciples plucked heads of grain and ate the food raw. Some Pharisees took exception to this, seeing it as grinding and therefore *working*! Jesus reminded them of David and the importance of the heart of the law. How easy it is, as the Lord tells us, to 'strain out a gnat and swallow a camel!' (Matt. 23:24).

The disciples were willing to eat whatever food came to hand. The law itself allowed the poor to take from a field what they could eat as they passed. It was not considered theft, for the very same reason that sustaining life is more important than mere ritual. Christ reminded his hearers that he is 'Lord of the Sabbath' (Luke 6:5). His interpretation of how we should conduct ourselves on the Sabbath day is therefore paramount.

On another occasion, Jesus entered a synagogue and taught. A man with a withered hand was there. The Lord could easily have left him one more day in that condition. Yet he desired to show mercy there and then—and mercy is at the heart of the law.

Mark very specifically recorded the righteous anger which our Lord felt at that moment (Mark 3:5). Then Jesus healed the man. Some say the only healings the Lord performed were to people who requested the healing and who had faith that healing would occur—yet here the man did not ask for his hand to be healed, and there is no mention that he had strong faith. As in the raising of the dead, so, here, Christ exercised his sovereign power as he chose.

Notice the intense dislike of the Lord and his methods that we encounter in these verses (Luke 6:7, 11). Matthew and Mark tell us that these religious leaders wanted to kill him. How strange are the hearts of men!

FOR FURTHER STUDY

1. See Luke 6:1. Landowners in Old Testament times had to leave part of their crops for the poor. They were permitted to take as much as they needed at that time, but were not to take a sickle to it or abuse the kindness shown (Deut. 23:25; 24:19-22). With this principle in mind, what provision for the poor could be made today?

2. Read Luke 6:1-12. What does Isaiah 58:13, 14 teach us about the relationship between delighting in the Sabbath and delighting in God?
3. Christ expressed righteous anger more than once. Consider the context of the following verses: Mark 3:5; John 2:13-17; Psalm 2:12; Revelation 6:15-17.

TO THINK ABOUT AND DISCUSS

1. Consider Luke 6:5. What are the benefits we enjoy from a well-spent Sunday? Are we too rigid or too lenient about observing the Lord's Day today?
2. The Pharisees were concerned about small matters but neglected the more important matters of justice, mercy and faith (Matt. 23:23). Do we have this tendency?

Choosing his friends (6:12-16)

There is nothing haphazard in our Lord's choice of followers. The Lord spent the night in prayer to God before their official call to serve him in this way. The choice of these men would be crucial to the establishing of the church and the fulfilment of prophecy.

The next day he called twelve[4] disciples. We know from chapter five of Luke's Gospel that James, John, Peter and Matthew had already been called to follow him. Now the Lord was officially ordaining them to the task of discipleship. A 'disciple' in the scriptural sense is a 'learner' (Greek, 'mathetes'). A disciple goes on learning about his teacher. Jesus taught the twelve that those who are fully trained shall be 'like their teacher' (Luke 6:40). One day they would continue and develop the work begun by their Lord in teaching, preaching and healing. Their task would be to 'make disciples of all the nations' (Matt. 28:19).

Power to heal (6:17-19)

People were willing to travel many miles from the south (Judaea) and the northwest (Tyre) in order to be healed. This account tells us of the 'power' (Greek, 'dynamis') that went out from Christ to heal as people touched him (v. 19). Later, in Luke 8:43-48, Jesus could feel power leave his body. The power at work during his ministry was the same by which all things came into being (Col. 1:16, 17).

FOR FURTHER STUDY

1. See Luke 6:13-16. Note that the lists of disciples always begin with Peter and end with Judas Iscariot (see Matt. 10:2-4 and Mark 3:13-19). Why is this so?
2. Consider what we know about the twelve. There are three sets of brothers, one tax collector (Levi, or Matthew), one 'zealot'—Simon—who may well at one time have been a political agitator and at least one who used to be a disciple of John the Baptist (Andrew, see John 1:35-40). Some say that Bartholomew was in fact the surname of Nathanael. He was led to Christ by Philip (John 1:43-51). What else do we know about them?
3. See Luke 6:16. Two disciples had the name 'Judas', one being Judas Iscariot. Today the name is, of course, associated with betrayal and sin. At that time, however, the term Judas was simply a Greek form of 'Judah' and in the minds of their parents would have conjured up images of 'Judas Maccabaeus', the heroic military leader who ruled from 166 BC to 160 BC.
4. Look up Luke 6:17. Just how well known the Lord was at this time is difficult to determine. What is clear is that later on, Pontius Pilate had no clear knowledge of him (Luke 23:2), whereas Herod had both heard of him and desired that he perform a miracle (Luke 23:8).
5. How different was the power that went out from Jesus (v. 19) and that which he gave to his disciples? See Mark 3:14, 15 and Acts 3:12.

TO THINK ABOUT AND DISCUSS

1. Consider Luke 6:12, 13. How important is intense prayer before we make major decisions?
2. When Judas Iscariot hung himself, why was it necessary to appoint another disciple to make up the twelve? (See Acts 1:15-26.)
3. The term 'Christian' was a nickname given to disciples in the early years of the church (Acts 11:26). Would it be more helpful and accurate for us to speak of believers today as 'disciples'?
4. If the Lord Jesus made and sustains the whole universe by his power, does he demonstrate this any less today than during his ministry?

The sermon (6:20-49)

Introduction

Some of our Lord's hearers were in for a shock. Those who thought that, because he healed on the Sabbath, his principles concerning day-to-day conduct were relaxed and easygoing, had to think again. Here Jesus is hard-hitting, and a very high standard of holiness is set. We need to pray for grace and strength to live out these words day by day.

This sermon covers much the same ground as the Sermon on the Mount (Matt. 5-7). Some believe it to be Luke's version of that same sermon, and others, that it is a very similar address but preached on a different occasion. I take the latter view. There are many differences between them, not least the fact that this sermon was preached at the foot of a hill, in a 'level place' (Luke 6:17), whereas Matthew 5:1 describes the location as the top of a mountain. Luke contains 'woes' (vv. 24-26), not found in Matthew 5-7. The most famous difference is that Christ says, 'Blessed are you poor' (v. 20) rather than 'poor *in spirit*' (Matt. 5:3). No doubt the Lord preached many messages of this kind, covering the same themes, though expressed in slightly different ways.

The sermon begins

To understand our Lord's words, it is vital to notice that he was speaking to his followers; 'he lifted up his eyes toward his disciples, and said…' (v. 20). Christ teaches us that poor disciples, those who follow him regardless of the hardships and suffering, are blessed. Such people, whom the world regards as powerless and rejected, receive favour from God. The Saviour brought the gospel to the poor first (Luke 4:18), and 'the common people heard him gladly' (Mark 12:37).

Jesus called them 'blessed', that is, essentially 'happy', for they had been blessed by God. Most of the rewards were to be in the future, except for the reward granted to poor disciples. They were blessed *then* by being members of God's kingdom (v. 20).

The rich, the full, those who rejoiced in their power and popularity were, in fact, going to suffer. They had had their reward here on earth. They had received whatever pleasure or consolation they would ever have (see James 5:1, 2, 5). The words of Abraham to the rich man in hell are truly sobering (Luke 16:25). Christ elsewhere teaches that the rich *can* be saved, though it is very difficult for them (Mark 10:25-27).

The Lord wanted his followers to see that material prosperity, centred as it is upon earthly pleasures, can rob us of spiritual happiness.

Love for those who hate us: (6:27-36)

We are in a 'dog-eat-dog' society. So much of what we do is based upon self, pride and blind loyalties... We must love enemies, bless those who curse us and freely pass on goods to those who demand them or borrow them from us.

Here again, the general rules by which most of us live must be broken. This world is fallen, and most of its inhabitants bear grudges and hate their enemies. We are in a 'dog-eat-dog' society. So much of what we do is based upon self, pride and blind loyalties. Yet, instead of accommodating his teaching to the evil of our hearts, the Master attacked that evil. We must love enemies, bless those who curse us and freely pass on goods to those who demand them or borrow them from us. How many of us are willing to take Jesus' words seriously?

It is true that 'the wicked borrows and does not repay'; however, 'the righteous shows mercy and gives' (Ps. 37:21). This standard is hard to maintain, especially since the Lord is addressing poor followers whose possessions would be precious. Yet God's standard of true holiness has always been very high. True 'godliness' is 'God-likeness'. God 'is kind to the unthankful and evil...he is merciful' (vv. 35, 36) and the same should be true of us.

FOR FURTHER STUDY

1. Luke 6:20, 21, 24, 25. Examine carefully the following texts as they relate to spiritual and material poverty: Luke 16:19-23; James 2:1-5; Revelation 2:9; 3:17. What conclusions do you draw?
2. Luke 6:27-36. On the subject of forgiveness, consider this: in Matthew's account of the Lord's Prayer, the one petition Christ emphasizes at the conclusion is forgiveness (Matt. 6:14, 25). Perhaps that is our weakest point. Just as at the end of the Ten Commandments it is idolatry, the besetting sin of Israel, that is rebuked (Exod. 20:22, 23).
3. Luke 6:27-36. David seemed to forgive Shimei who cursed and threw stones at him (2 Sam. 16:5-12) yet later he called for his death (1 Kings 2:8, 9). What does this teach us about forgiveness?
4. Luke 6:27-36. Consider the reasons our Saviour gives for showing kindness to enemies. In what ways did Jesus himself live this way? See Luke 22:49-51, 63-65; 23:9-11, 34.

TO THINK ABOUT AND DISCUSS

1. Do the 'woes' in Luke 6:24-26 apply today to most of us in the West?
2. Considering Luke 6:24-26, how far do earthly pleasures rob us of spiritual happiness?
3. If someone were to say, 'Luke 6:27-36 teaches us to be doormats,' how should we answer?
4. In reading these words, we should ask, are we more like the 'sinners' described in Luke 6:32-34 or like God (Luke 6:35-36)?

'Judge not'…'Condemn not' (6:37, 41-42)

Once a person has attained any degree of obedience to God, the next pitfall is pride and a feeling of superiority. Yet the believer is not to judge others, particularly unbelievers. Paul tells us that there is a place for judging those who claim to follow Christ, but believers are not at liberty to judge outsiders (1 Cor. 5:11-13). The Lord teaches that if we desire to be forgiven, then we must forgive. How can we, who have been forgiven so much, bear grudges, and make others 'pay' for the injuries they have inflicted upon us?

In the unforgettable example of the speck of dust in the eye (vv. 41, 42), Jesus used hyperbole to make his point. A speck of sawdust is nowhere near as troublesome as a plank in the eye. Christ does not say we can never help our brother to overcome sin; but we must first deal with our own shortcomings.

In the unforgettable example of the speck of dust in the eye (vv. 41, 42), Jesus used hyperbole to make his point. A speck of sawdust is nowhere near as troublesome as a plank in the eye. Christ does not say we can never help our brother to overcome sin; but we must first deal with our own shortcomings.

'Give, and it will be given to you' (6:38)

This principle has been lived out by many. Those who have done so, such as J Hudson Taylor, George Müller and C T Studd, have declared not only the immense joy of giving, but also the delight of receiving daily supplies to meet all their needs. God is no one's debtor, and those who give freely of what they have will be rewarded by him.

Talk is cheap (6:43-49)

Fruitless trees are of no interest to God. In this sense the church is an orchard, not a forest. To be zealous, active and yet spiritually barren is to fall seriously short of God's standard. Elsewhere, the apostle Paul refers to this fruit as the evidence of the work of the Holy Spirit in our lives (Gal. 5:22, 23). Additionally, the Lord speaks of the connection between our heart and our words (v. 45). Idle and corrupt language teaches us a lot about the condition of a person's 'heart', that is, the centre of his or her affections and desires.

The two kinds of builders in Luke 6:46-49 are not described as 'wise' and 'foolish' as in Matthew 7. Instead, it is left to the reader to consider which one best represents him or her. In both cases, there are floods and streams which beat against the structure, perhaps speaking of the day of judgement, or else of afflictions and trials in general. Christ is saying here that to call him 'Lord' implies strict obedience to his will. We must never confuse fine or reverent words with true active obedience to our Lord's words.

FOR FURTHER STUDY

1. Luke 6:39-42: Consider these words in relation to Romans 2:1, 17-25. In what ways do we fail to see our own 'religious' arrogance and blindness?
2. Luke 6:45: Matthew's Gospel teaches us that our words are not only an indication of the condition of our heart, but the words themselves will be judged by God (Matt. 12:34-37).
3. Luke 6:45: Some never apply the adjective 'good' to a person. Certainly no human being is without sin. Yet are we at liberty to do so in the light of Luke 6:45, Romans 15:14 and Titus 1:8? What must be meant by this expression?
4. Luke 6:46-49: A correct understanding of what is meant by the word 'Lord' would help to explain just how committed a disciple should be. Try to find out the full meaning of this word in the New Testament (see John 13:13-15).

TO THINK ABOUT AND DISCUSS

1. Would we give more generously if we really took Luke 6:38 to heart? Should we expect financial blessings in return, or might they come in another form?
2. Consider Luke 6:43. Do we mistake doctrinal knowledge for 'fruit'?
3. See Luke 6:43. How much 'bad' fruit would a person have to bear before we should doubt his or her salvation?
4. Refer to Luke 6:47-49. Times of hard testing and the day of judgement will reveal what kind of a house we have built. Is it easier to tell who is obedient to Christ when we are in crisis?

7 Luke Chapter 7

How foolish it is when we judge others by their appearance! The Lord Jesus helped anyone who came to him, however unpopular his or her lifestyle or occupation was.

A centurion who believed (7:1-10)

The Roman soldiers were hated, and their army of occupation despised, yet there were Roman soldiers who respected Judaism. This centurion was a caring man, who desired his servant to be healed, and had demonstrated interest in Jewish worship of the true God (v. 5). Neither they nor the Lord judged this man by his clothes, his culture, or the life-and-death politics of the time.

The conversation that followed proves this point even more. Jesus began to walk to the centurion's home. Yet the centurion regarded himself as unworthy to receive Jesus under his roof. He described the way in which others obeyed him without question (v. 8). How great his faith! The Lord remarked that such faith had not been seen 'even in Israel!' (v. 9). The servant was healed at that same time, indicating Christ's power to heal at a distance from the patient.

Beauty for ashes (7:11-17).

Nain exists today as a small hamlet some five miles from Nazareth. A crowd had gathered there for the funeral of a young man. In this whole account our Lord's thoughts were with the grieving mother. This widow was in the same position as Naomi in the book of Ruth, having lost both husband and son. This widow's son was not only loved as a person, but he would have represented her joy, her strength and her future. Reaching into her despair, Christ touched the open bier or stretcher and said to her son, 'Young man, I say to you, arise.' The young man sat up immediately. It is wonderful to imagine the overwhelming joy and relief that must have flooded the hearts of those who had been grieving yet now saw the young man alive and well!

The rest of the crowd were fearful, and glorified God. Luke is careful not to put words into the people's mouths—they do not recite the full list of our Lord's attributes. Instead, in their own language, subject to their own understanding they said 'A great prophet has risen up among us' and 'God has visited his people' (v. 16).

A prophet with questions (7:18-35)

John had been in Herod's dungeon for a long time. The man who from his youth was accustomed to living in the wide and rocky expanses of the wilderness was now confined to a cell. Jesus, whom he knew to be the Messiah, had helped and healed a vast number of people. If he, as Messiah, had come to proclaim 'liberty to the captives' (Luke 4:18), then why was his forerunner left to suffer in a dungeon? This caused John serious difficulties. He therefore sent to Christ to ask a question, 'Are you the Coming One, or do we look for another?' (v. 19). Jesus, with broad brush strokes, characterized his ministry (v. 22). What is mentioned last seems emphasized most: 'The poor have the gospel preached to them'. Our Lord saw to it that hungry crowds were fed by loaves and fish; yet he emphasized that his greatest gift to the poor is the gospel. Next, the Lord, far from condemning John's question, spoke more highly of him than of any man who has ever lived (v. 28). He pointed out, however, that even those who were 'least in the kingdom of God' were greater than John. It seems the Lord may have meant that the very least of the saints in glory, without sin and perfected, was greater than John.

Our Lord saw to it that hungry crowds were fed by loaves and fish; yet he emphasized that his greatest gift to the poor is the gospel.

He pointed out that John came as the rugged messenger of God, fulfilling Malachi 3:1. Here the truth brought division; the tax collectors who had been baptized by John 'justified' God, that is, proclaimed him righteous. The Pharisees and lawyers, however, 'rejected the will of God for themselves', and had refused his baptism.

Next Christ compared the people of that generation to children calling upon each other to dance or mourn. He implied here (vv. 31-35) that whatever God's people do, there will be people who find fault and criticize them. Yet the Lord refused to bow to the pressures around him.

FOR FURTHER STUDY

1. Consider to what extent it is true that, when given the truth, pagans believe sooner and more deeply than those raised in a spiritual community (see Ezek. 3:4-7; Rom. 15:20, 21).
2. How far does God's Word overcome prejudice about other nations and individuals? Consider Rahab (Josh. 2:8-11), Nebuchadnezzar (Dan. 4:34-37), and the people of Nineveh (Jonah 3:4-10; 4:11).
3. Refer to Luke 7:22. How often when lists are given in the Bible, do we find the last item is placed there for emphasis? See Proverbs 6:16-19; 30:18, 19.
4. Our Saviour points out the virtues of becoming like little children (Matt. 18:3). However, the New Testament also warns us not to be childish and immature (Luke 7:31, 32; 1 Cor. 13:11; Eph. 4:14). Can you explain the distinction between these two approaches? Please give examples.

TO THINK ABOUT AND DISCUSS

1. How important is it for those who are sick to be physically touched by those who pray for them? (See 2 Kings 5:9-12 and John 9:6, 7.)
2. To what extent should ministry to widows be a priority in today's church? (See James 1:27.)
3. 'A great prophet has risen up among us' (v. 16). How much understanding of the person and work of the Lord Jesus is necessary to salvation?
4. In view of John's question (v. 19), how far can discouragement weaken faith?
5. See Luke 7:31, 32. In what ways does the world today try to get us to 'dance to its tune'? When might the world mourn and we rejoice?
6. Look up Luke 7:33-35. To what extent should a Christian expect his behaviour to be misinterpreted by the world?

'Sinners—keep out' (7:36-50)

The Lord was dining with a Pharisee. A woman, who was a 'sinner', came into the house. She was well-known for her sinful life, perhaps as a prostitute. She had with her an alabaster flask of oil. In biblical times, fragrant oil was considered of great value.[5] This woman, without thought for the expense of her gift, cracked open the flask of oil. She anointed Jesus, washed his feet with her tears, and dried them with her hair.

Those around seemed unmoved by the spectacle. They merely wondered why Jesus, if a prophet, had failed to detect her true character. Yet the Lord intended to teach a powerful lesson through her. He gave a short parable of two men who owed money—one owed five hundred denarii, and the other fifty. When both debts were cancelled, which would love the most? The answer is, the man who owed the most. So it is with sinners. This woman, aware as she was of her wickedness and sin, owed more to God than others, and yet, once forgiven, would demonstrate more love. Therefore the Lord said to the woman, 'Your sins are forgiven' and later, 'your faith has saved you'.

What she had done was kinder and more considerate even than Simon who had invited Jesus to his home. She had demonstrated more love, more devotion and more gratitude than the Pharisee. The reason for this? She was aware of a greater debt of gratitude to her Saviour. How great is your debt to him?

FOR FURTHER STUDY

1. Consider Luke 7:36-50. There are other cases where Christ is similarly anointed. What particular features of these accounts do we notice?
2. Look up Luke 7:37, 38. Does strong faith give people a measure of audacity? (See Luke 5:18-20; Luke 8:43-48.)
3. Refer to Luke 7:39, 40. Clearly Jesus knew the thoughts of others (see Luke 6:7, 8). What does this tell us about his knowledge of people? See John 2:25.

TO THINK ABOUT AND DISCUSS

1. Refer to Luke 7:39. Does familiarity with the commandments of God make us hard-hearted toward sinners?
2. Should churches make a special effort to reach the worst sinners, and welcome them enthusiastically to their church meetings, knowing that (if saved) they would love the Lord more than respectable people?

8 Luke Chapter 8

It has been asked, particularly since we never read of him asking for money, how the ministry of Christ was financed. In part, this question is answered here.

Women who sustained the ministry (8:1-3)

These women and others alluded to here 'provided for him from their substance' (v. 3). Among the women listed is Joanna, the wife of Chuza, Herod's steward. She probably had a comfortable income, and would have given freely to assist Jesus' ministry.

However, there never seemed to be a great surplus of wealth, since as is recorded at the beginning of Luke 6, Christ and his disciples went through the fields plucking heads of grain for food. It must also be noted that at our Lord's death, all he had in his possession for the Roman soldiers to gamble over was a single set of clothes.

The Parable of the Sower (8:4-18)

Here is one of our Lord's best-known parables. When the gospel is presented, not everyone instantly believes, and not all people instantly reject what they hear—in fact, of the four cases given, three of them seem promising, at least at the beginning!

Christ explained that the seed is the word of God. There is nothing wrong with the seed. Nor did Jesus suggest that the sower should share any blame for failure of growth. So it is whenever the word of God is proclaimed; the word is pure; the motives of the evangelist or preacher may be of the highest standard; yet still not all listeners will believe and bear fruit.

Some of the seed lands on stony ground (v. 13). Such people love to hear the word read or preached, yet they have no depth of earth and fall away. Some find that cares, riches and pleasures, like weeds, choke them, and 'they bring no fruit to maturity' (v. 14).

The final group comprise those who receive the word of God on good ground, and with 'a noble and good heart' eventually bear fruit with perseverance.

In the middle of this passage, Jesus explained the purpose of parables: they were to reveal the truth to God's people, but also to conceal truth from the world (vv. 9, 10 and Isa. 6:9). Jesus did not thrust the meaning of parables upon those who heard him. When his disciples asked him to explain the meaning, he would do so, as in verse 9.

'Take heed how you hear' (v. 18). How important it is, as our Lord stressed at the end of chapter 6, to hear and obey the words of God. We dare not ignore God or take his truth casually. Our eternal future is affected by our response to what we hear from God.

Family ties (8:19-21).

When children were brought to the Lord, it surprised the disciples to see how willingly he gave up time to bless them. It must have shocked the disciples, however, to see how sternly the Messiah dealt with his own mother and half-brothers. Yet our Lord was establishing a principle—that all who hear the word of God and obey it are accounted members of his family (v. 21).

FOR FURTHER STUDY

1. The world contains people at many different stages of spiritual life. Some, like a scribe Jesus met, are 'not far from the kingdom of God' (Mark 12:34). Some appear saved, yet persevere only for a short time. Yet when the Messiah returns, there will be only two kinds of people (see Matt. 25:31-33). How can you explain this?
2. The parable of the sower reveals that many people begin well, yet bring forth no fruit. In the early church those who said they believed were received into the church very quickly (see Acts 2 and 5). Yet if their lives were consistently sinful, they were to be disciplined and cast out of the church (see Acts 2:41, 46, 47 and compare 1 Cor. 5:11-13). Should we do the same?
3. 'Parables were given by the Lord as much to *conceal* the truth as to *reveal* it'. Is this true in the light of Isaiah 6:9 and Luke 8:9, 10?
4. How far can we say that God is sovereign not only in salvation, but in every area of spiritual enlightenment? (See 2 Kings 6:15-17 and Acts 13:48; 16:14.)
5. Look again at Luke 8:2, 3. How important is it that Christian workers are supported financially, to free them to serve God? (See 1 Cor. 9:7-14.) Why did Paul sometimes refuse this help (1 Cor. 9:15-18)?

TO THINK ABOUT AND DISCUSS

1. The parable of the sower reveals that of the many types of people in the world, true believers will sooner or later bear fruit. Does this parable therefore teach us to wait for fruit before baptizing people?
2. Luke 8:14. Are Christians vulnerable throughout their lives to the choking effect of 'cares, riches and pleasures'?
3. Considering Luke 8:19-21, do you think Lucien of Antioch (an early Christian believer) was correct when he said, 'A Christian's only relatives are the saints'?
3. Do we give cheerfully and sacrificially to those in full-time Christian service?

Christ's power (8:22-56)

In the verses which remain in this chapter, we see Christ's power over wind and waves, over demons, sickness and even over death.

Power over creation (8:22-25)

It is easy to say we have faith when all is well and our feet are firmly on the ground. Yet when times of trial come, our faith can be tested to its limits. When we are in dire straits, where do we look? How steadfast is our confidence and faith in God?

The Lord had commanded the disciples to sail across the Sea of Galilee, a distance of perhaps several miles.[6] A storm arose and the boat was tossed to and fro by the waves. These were days before radio distress signals, and there was no one to call upon but God. Yet even in such circumstances, we find the Saviour fast asleep. More than merely being the sleep of exhaustion, it indicated a deep trust in the protecting care of his Father in heaven. By contrast, the disciples were afraid, and in their anxiety called out to the Lord; 'Master, master, we are perishing' (v. 24) or as Mark puts it, 'Teacher, do you not care that we are perishing?' (Mark 4:38). Jesus stood up and rebuked the wind and the raging water. They were astounded at his power over the elements. He demonstrated again his divine authority, and challenged their lack of faith.

Power over demons (8:26-39)

As Jesus arrived in Gadara, he came across a man who lived among tombs. He was an outcast, having a 'legion' of demons within him. In Roman armies, a 'legion' consisted of 6,000 men, indicating that this man had a vast number of evil spirits within him. We might say that from a human perspective he seemed beyond cure. When we speak glibly of the influence of Satan, it would be a good idea to think about this man. Satan removes our joy; he wounds and destroys. Yet the Lord has far greater power.

The demons speak words of truth to the Lord, calling him 'Jesus, son of the most high God'. It seems that they feared most of all being sent into the 'abyss'.[7] The Lord allows them to enter a herd of about 2,000 pigs (Mark 5:13—which again indicates the number of demons involved) which rush into the sea and are drowned.

Afterwards we find the man 'sitting at the feet of Jesus, clothed and in his right mind'. What a beautiful picture of what it means to be not only healed, but filled with gratitude and delight in the Lord.

In the verses that follow we see a whole variety of

responses to the Saviour and his ministry:

FEAR: The people were frightened (vv. 35b, 37) and they ask the Lord to depart from them. There is a contrast between the spiritual mind and the mind only informed by this world. Those who are outside of the kingdom prefer to choose their own way of life, and be left alone.

DESIRE TO FOLLOW: The man asked if he could follow Jesus, but he was told to return to his own people and tell them the great things God had done for him (v. 39). This he accomplished with great zeal as the whole city was told of what Christ had done for him.

JOY: The people on the other side of the Sea of Galilee gladly received him, for they were all anxiously waiting for him (v. 40). Among them were two particular people, desperate for immediate help.

Power over sickness and death (8:40-56)

Luke gives us an insight into the fragmented and busy life of Christ as he ministered to the needs of others. Jairus, a ruler of the synagogue, asked Christ to come into his house for he had a twelve-year-old daughter who was dying. We feel something of Jairus' agony and helplessness as we are told he 'fell down at Jesus' feet and begged him to come to his house.'

The Lord made his way toward the house, and the crowd 'thronged him'. A woman who, for twelve years had suffered haemorrhaging, approached him. All her money had been spent on doctors' fees, yet she could not be healed. Mark tells us that her condition had grown worse over time (Mark 5:26). During these years she would have lived as an outcast (Lev. 15:25-27).

Rather than ask the Lord directly for healing, the woman approached Jesus and touched the 'border', or hem of his garment. This border was worn by Jewish people to remind them of God's laws (Num. 15:37-40). Luke, himself a doctor, describes her flow of blood as immediately 'stanched' (v. 44, AV). The Saviour asked, 'Who touched me?' He knew that someone had been healed, for he felt power leave his body. What Jesus wanted, it seems, was a public declaration of what had been done for her. How important it is when we receive blessing to tell others, that they may also give glory to God.

News then came that Jairus' daughter was dead. At that moment, many might have wondered why the Lord had visited Gadara a short while before, or why it was that the woman who was just healed had slowed down the group on their way to Jairus' home. Yet God, who knows and ordains all things, intended to reveal his power on this occasion by resurrection rather than healing!

News then came that Jairus' daughter was dead. At that moment, many might have wondered why the Lord had visited Gadara a short while before, or why it was that the woman who was just healed had slowed down the group on their way to Jairus' home. Yet God, who knows and ordains all things, intended to reveal his power on this occasion by resurrection rather than healing!

Christ took his inner circle of three disciples, Peter, James and John, and entered the room. Jesus was no showman during his ministry, and did not want the applause of a crowd as the girl came to life. As when Elijah and Elisha raised two children to life, this resurrection was to occur privately. The *fact* of the raising of this child mattered more than the number of people who saw it.

The Saviour spoke to the girl. For a moment, just ponder how strange it is to tell a dead person to 'rise up', as when the Lord called dead Lazarus to 'come forth' (John 11:43). Yet life is given at the moment the words are spoken, and with that life the ability to hear the command itself. So it is with salvation—life comes to the sinner as the word of God is spoken and the sinner responds by trusting in Christ. The girl's life is restored, and the Lord calmly directs her family to give her something to eat.

FOR FURTHER STUDY

1. How often do Satan and the demons mix truth with lies? Consider this in the light of Genesis 3:4, 5; Luke 4:34, 41 and Acts 16:16, 17.

2. See Luke 8:28. The demons anticipated with horror the day of judgement (see Matt. 8:29). Do we anticipate it as vividly?

3. Consider Luke 8:51. Why were Peter, James and John chosen to be with the Lord at key moments of his ministry—the transfiguration, the raising of Jairus' daughter, the Lord's prayer at Gethsemane, etc?

4. Read Luke 8:54, 55. Christ specifically raised three people to life in the Gospels: Jairus' daughter (Luke 8:49); the widow of Nain's son (Luke 7:12) and Lazarus (John 11:43). Look up the circumstances of each occasion and the reaction of the people;

note that in the raising of Lazarus the response was most fierce (John 11:57; 12:10,11).

5. Consider Luke 8:56. Why were Jairus and his wife told to tell no one of this healing? See Luke 5:14, 15; 9:21.

TO THINK ABOUT AND DISCUSS

1. Look up Luke 8:33. The man had been self-destructive, and later the herd of swine killed themselves. How far are those who contemplate suicide influenced by Satan?

2. Why did the people want the Saviour to leave (v. 37)?

3. In the light of Luke 8:39, explain how important it is for us to proclaim the gospel to those of our own family and community.

4. See Luke 8:43, 44 and 2 Chronicles 16:12, 13. Are we too swift to go for medical help when we are unwell? Is prayer for recovery too far down the list?

5. How important is public testimony to healing?

9 Luke Chapter 9

The relationship of the disciples to Jesus, as we see from Luke chapters 8-10, might be visualized as follows: Jesus at the centre of a series of concentric circles—closest to him are Peter, James and John, then the rest of the twelve, next the seventy strong adherents (sent out in Luke 10:1-16), and finally the five thousand who were fed miraculously in Galilee (Luke 9:10-17).

Sent out (9:1-6)

Luke 9 begins with what may seem to us a daunting moment. The twelve disciples, who perhaps had only heard the Lord's teaching for a matter of weeks, were sent out. Their task was twofold, 'to preach the kingdom of God and to heal the sick' (v. 2). Jesus directed them as follows:

They were not to go out in their own strength. The Lord only sent them out after he had given them 'power and authority over all demons, and to cure diseases'. They went two by two (Mark 6:7). Perhaps this was in order for them to support each other, and to demonstrate love as evidence of their discipleship (John 13:35).

They were not to rely on their own resources (v. 3), deliberately stripping themselves of any material supports such as a staff for protection or a bag of money for security. They were not even permitted to take extra clothing. The Lord wanted his disciples to learn to trust in God for everything, just as he had taught them (Matt. 6:25-30).

They were to learn to accept the kindness of those who took them into their homes. The apostle Paul expected widows in the church to offer hospitality even to 'strangers' (1 Tim. 5:10).

The disciples had to be harsh with those communities which rejected their message. They were not just quietly to leave the town or village that rejected the truth, but had to testify against them, shaking off the dust from their feet.

The disciples obeyed, and later testified of the goodness of the Lord to them. When asked much later if they lacked anything during this time of preaching and healing, there is power in their answer. They lacked 'nothing' (Luke 22:35). Isn't it wonderful to see the lessons of trust our Lord was teaching them even at this early stage in their spiritual development!

A ruler seeks Jesus (9:7-9)

Herod, in what seems to be a strange mixture of guilt and curiosity, wanted to see the Messiah. Was this indeed the prophet he had executed risen from the dead? Whatever his motives, and however great his power, he was unable to see him. Jesus had little time for those who wanted to see him for vain and empty reasons. Later on, in Luke 13:31, 32, Jesus refused to be intimidated by Herod. Later still, he would stand silent before this idle ruler, whose malicious guard would treat him with contempt (Luke 23:6-12).

Food for all (9:10-17)

Jesus had listened to all the blessings the disciples had received during their travels. Now he seeks time alone with God. Christ felt the need for private prayer, yet did not use his love of prayer as a reason to turn the crowds away, but rather ministered to the crowds in exactly the same way as he had taught his disciples. In Luke 9:2 he told them to 'preach the kingdom of God and to heal the sick'. Here he 'spoke to them about the kingdom of God, and healed those who had need of healing' (v. 11).

As the day drew to its close, the Lord's disciples, who had come with the multitudes, suggested quite understandably that the people find lodging and food in the surrounding villages. What he wanted to teach them, however, was that the same provision they had received during their missionary journey was available to this vast crowd. The God who sustains the universe would provide. The disciples, who had been the means of healing and blessing to others, must now give food to this crowd (v. 13).

Taking just one meal, Christ multiplied the loaves and fish, and fed the whole crowd. Verse 16 shows how the Lord looked up to heaven, blessed and broke the loaves and fish. Twelve baskets of crumbs were left over, a further proof that nothing is too hard for the Lord. So important is this occurrence to our Lord's ministry that this incident is recorded in all four Gospels.

FOR FURTHER STUDY

1. Look up Luke 9:3. Consider the many examples in Scripture of those who have denied themselves material help in order to prove the power of God: Gideon's army reduced to three hundred (Judg. 7:3-7); David and the sling (1 Sam. 17:38-40); Ezra and a military guard (Ezra 8:21-23).
2. See Luke 9:3. How far can it be said that God rewards trust in him (see Ps. 37:39, 40)?
3. Consider Luke 9:3 further. It might be said, 'The church is always strongest when free from material wealth and earthly power'. Do you agree with this statement?
4. Look at Luke 9:16, 17. Elisha multiplied barley loaves and corn (2 Kings 4:42-44). What makes the miracle of Jesus so much greater?

TO THINK ABOUT AND DISCUSS

1. Luke 9:1-6. How important are years of formal training in a college for missionaries before they are sent out by a church? Are there other ways by which they can be equipped to serve God?
2. Consider Luke 9:3. How far do we expect missionaries to trust God for daily sustenance? Should we expect this of all Christians?

Who is Jesus? (9:18-36)

Here we learn a great deal about the identity of Christ, his mission and how we are to follow him. Until this point, the disciples only had hints of our Lord's true identity.

'Who do the crowds say that I am?' (vv. 18-20). Clearly there were similarities between the lifestyle and ministry of Jesus and that of the prophets. Yet the Lord was more interested in what his own followers thought of him: 'But who do *you* say that I am?' Peter showed that he knew a great deal about the identity of Jesus, calling him 'the Christ of God' (v. 20). 'Christ' is simply the Greek form of 'Messiah', the anointed messenger of God.

The suffering Messiah (9:21-22)

They were told to tell no one of this. Then Jesus referred to his death, saying he would be rejected by the religious leaders (v. 22), then killed and raised to life on the third day. Our Saviour was teaching that he would be a suffering Messiah. The scriptures must be fulfilled (Ps. 22; Isa. 53; Zech. 12:10, etc). The prophecies concerning his glorious earthly kingdom would be completely fulfilled, not at his first coming, but at the second.

Taking up the cross (9:23-26)

All who followed him were to take up their 'cross' each day and follow him. We must remember that the disciples had never heard before how it was that their Lord would die and this must have seemed a very strange way of speaking, perhaps rather like someone in more recent times saying, 'Take up your noose and follow me!' This language was intended to be obeyed, not just remembered. Only in Luke's account does the word 'daily' occur (v. 23). The disciple follows his Master moment by moment, day by day. Self-interest must not dominate the lives of believers. Instead, God's people have to be willing to suffer and to deny themselves every day, just as their Master.

Each day will bring its own share of burdens and

opportunities for suffering for the truth. At the end of the chapter (vv. 57-62), the practical implications of these words are seen, as people who were willing to share the *excitement* of our Lord's ministry drew back from its hardships.

Have you begun to follow the Lord Jesus in this way? Are you ready to face hardships and to speak boldly of him? We must ask ourselves these questions. The Lord proceeded with the poignant question, 'What profit is it to a man if he gains the whole world, and is himself destroyed or lost?' (v. 25). To gain this world's money, power or popularity is meaningless if final judgement swallows you up. Here Christ was speaking of the temptation to avoid persecution and pain. To be ashamed of Christ or of his words will mean that he also will be ashamed of us (v. 26). Our Lord's hearers would have to speak up for Christ in the face of severe persecution, and even death.

Jesus seen clearly (9:27-36)

Some were there present who would see the kingdom of God before they 'tasted death'. It may be that our Lord was here referring to the transfiguration. At that moment, the true glory of the Messiah was seen—for Jesus represents the kingdom of heaven. It was said, as he entered Jerusalem on Palm Sunday, 'Blessed is the kingdom of our father David that comes in the name of the Lord!' (Mark 11:10). This could also be implied in Jesus' words, 'The kingdom of God is within you' (Luke 17:20, 21), which may be translated 'in the midst of you'.

The Lord took Peter, James and John up a mountain—possibly Mount Hermon or Mount Tabor, but the precise location is unknown. As Jesus was praying, his face became bright and his clothes shone. Moses and Elijah, representative of the law and the prophets, stood on either side of Jesus, a symbolic display that the Lord Jesus fulfilled the Old Testament by his life, death and resurrection. Moses and Elijah spoke specifically of his death (v. 31). The entire sacrificial system under Moses pointed to the perfect sacrifice of the Saviour.

Though surrounded by the glory of Christ, the disciples became heavy with sleep. This occurred at other times in the Scriptures, strange as it may seem to us.

Peter desired to make three tabernacles, or booths, in order that the Lord, Moses and Elijah might remain there. How often we desire to maintain a beautiful spiritual experience! Yet the Lord teaches us that there comes a time when we must move on. A cloud overshadowed them, and a voice spoke in a similar way to the day of our Lord's baptism, except that the emphasis here is on his teaching: 'This is my beloved son, hear him' (v. 35). After the voice, Christ stood alone with his disciples.

FOR FURTHER STUDY

1. What elements of our Lord's teaching would have led people to conclude he might be John the Baptist, Elijah or one of the old prophets (v. 19)?

2. How did people view the coming of the 'Christ' or 'Messiah'? See for instance Daniel 9:25, 26 and John 4:25, 26.

3. How significant was the appearance of Moses and Elijah in the transfiguration?

4. To us, a visitation from God would be remarkable—we imagine it would be enough

to wake us up! Yet in Scripture there are instances of believers becoming overwhelmed with sleep even in the midst of a spectacular vision (see Dan. 8:18; 10:7-9). Why is this?

TO THINK ABOUT AND DISCUSS

1. The clear meaning and implications of verses 22, 23 and 44 seem very obvious to us today. Why were these things 'hidden' from the disciples (v. 45)?
2. Consider Luke 9:45. Are there prophecies of Scripture, yet to be fulfilled, which have been 'hidden' from us today?
3. What is the real meaning of denying ourselves and taking up the cross today (v. 23)?
4. Look at Luke 9:26. In what circumstances might a modern believer be considered 'ashamed' of Christ's words?

The descent (9:37-42)

It is the frequent experience of God's people that 'mountaintop' experiences are followed by times of discouragement. The Lord came down to face a dispute. A boy was in danger of serious injury from convulsions brought on by a demon, yet the Lord's disciples could not heal him—causing the Son of God to cry out, 'O faithless and perverse generation' (v. 41). Jesus was more grieved by the doubts of others than anyone else we read of in Scripture. To the one who created the heavens and the earth, doubt was inexcusable. The Lord then drove out the demon, and handed the child to his father.

The disciples and their master (9:43-45)

Christ again spoke of his death, revealing that his sufferings would begin with betrayal. He told the disciples to remember these sayings; they were to 'sink down into your ears' (v. 44). The disciples were not able to understand this saying, for 'it was hidden from them' (v. 45). Fear also kept them from bringing up the subject. Later, the Holy Spirit would help them to remember his words (John 16:12, 13). Just how well the disciples were later enabled to remember the Lord's teaching is revealed in the detailed and accurate way they penned the Gospels.

Attitudes to insiders (9:46-48)

The disciples seemed to have an ongoing debate as to who was the greatest. This may have sprung up over the Lord's choice of Peter, James and John to witness his transfiguration (vv. 28-36). Could it be that these three were the greatest of all? Whatever the content of their discussion, Jesus ended it abruptly, perceiving the 'thought of their heart' and teaching them that he, their Lord, happily identified with a little child. Anyone who received that child received him and those who received Christ received the Father who had sent him.

Few adults would be happy to identify so readily with a toddler. We like to be thought of as wise and mature—yet the Lord taught the importance of humility. Are we willing to be last and least?

Our attitude to outsiders (9:49-56)

John, here the spokesman for the disciples, mentioned a situation that had already occurred. A man had been driving out demons in the name of Jesus. This seemed to be misusing the Lord's name, and he might be considered a rival. However, Jesus made the point that the man was not to be forbidden to work in this way (v. 50)—he proclaimed Christ. By our Lord's response, it is evident that he wanted the disciples to be aware of an important truth early on in their spiritual lives: One day the kingdom, which began with the twelve as a small brook, would gradually widen as a flowing river, to encompass all believing people from the nations.

> The disciples seemed to have an ongoing debate as to who was the greatest. This may have sprung up over the Lord's choice of Peter, James and John ... Whatever the content of their discussion, Jesus ended it abruptly, perceiving the 'thought of their heart' and teaching them that he, their Lord, happily identified with a little child.

Next, Jesus had to deal with a loveless response to unbelief. He had 'set his face' to go to Jerusalem. He had mentioned his impending sufferings a few times in recent days. Yet far from making him change the course of his life, he knew it must be in Jerusalem that his life would be offered up. Messengers were sent ahead to prepare for his arrival in the surrounding villages. A Samaritan village would not entertain Jesus because of his desire to travel to Jerusalem. A deep rift had grown between the Jews and the Samaritans (see comments on Luke 10:25-37).

James and John were two disciples whom the Lord had previously nicknamed 'sons of thunder' (Mark 3:17), perhaps because of their impulsiveness. The two brothers desired to see fire come down from heaven and consume the unbelievers, just as in the days of Elijah (2 Kings 1:9-15). In their zeal for the reputation of Christ, they had failed to learn the lesson of love. His kingdom expands today as it always has done through love, not hatred; by the weapon of the Scriptures, not by the gun. If only everyone who claimed to know Christ had learned this simple lesson taught to James and John: 'the Son of Man did not come to destroy men's lives but to save them' (v. 56).

The true cost of discipleship (9:57-62)

Some people imagine that the ministry of the Lord Jesus was a frantic quest for followers but these verses refute this view. Jesus would accept anyone who came to him on his terms. He would not make discipleship sound attractive to the flesh; he did not mislead people into a rosy view of what it meant to be a first-century follower of Christ.

Before we judge any of these people too harshly for seeming to turn back, we must ask, 'Would we have been willing to be homeless or to sever ties with our families at a moment's notice?' Few of us have perhaps really comprehended the degree of self-sacrifice that Christ expects from his followers.

The first (vv. 57, 58) was eager to follow the Lord, but it

seems that homelessness was too great an obstacle to him. The second (vv. 59, 60) wanted first to bury his father. It may be that the man was gravely ill, and required him to stay longer, or that his father was already dead—yet even a day's delay was too long for our Lord. The man was to begin at that instant to 'preach the kingdom of God'.

The last (vv. 61, 62) wanted to bid his family 'goodbye'. When Elisha had asked for this long before, the request was granted (1 Kings 19:20). Yet here the Son of God wanted to teach the extreme importance of his message; it was more urgent even than Elijah's, and he could not wait. Eternity depended on it, and hesitation disqualified people from true service. Such a person was like a man driving a plough and not looking where he was going and beginning to plough uneven furrows.

FOR FURTHER STUDY

1. See Luke 9:37-41 and note how mountaintop experiences in Scripture are often followed by disappointment and discouragement. Look up Exodus 32:15-20 (Mount Sinai) and 1 Kings 19:4 (after Mount Carmel, when fire had come down from heaven). Such discouragements in our own experience should not surprise us.
2. Was the saying about his death hidden from the disciples (v. 45) in order for Judas to harden his heart, and the Scriptures to be fulfilled (Ps. 69:25; Ps. 109:8)?
3. How can we reconcile Luke 9:50 and Matthew 12:30?
4. Compare 2 Kings 1:9-15 and Luke 9:51-56. What is different about the urgency of following Christ, compared with following the prophet Elijah?
5. Consider Luke 9:57-62. Most of the twelve disciples died violently. We know from the Scriptures that Judas hanged himself. James the brother of John was beheaded (Acts 12:1, 2). The Lord told Peter that he would die as a martyr (John 21:18, 19). As for

the rest, we cannot be certain what happened to them at the end of their lives. Tradition says that all but John died as martyrs. Jesus was preparing them for fierce persecution.

TO THINK ABOUT AND DISCUSS

1. What lessons can we learn from children as we serve Christ? (See Luke 9:46-48). How can we 'receive them' (v. 48) in the terms which Christ meant in today's society? Look up Luke 9:49, 50. When does a church go too far in 'writing off' other believers whose approach or methods are different from theirs?

2. Consider Luke 9:51-56. Do believers ever feel hostile towards those who reject our message? How ought we to react?

3. Are we more committed to our relatives than to Christ? Discuss this in the light of Luke 9:59-62.

4. Should the expression 'Let the dead bury their own dead' (v. 60) affect the way we view funerals?

5. In the presentation of the gospel today, do we sufficiently stress the hardships of following Christ? Answer in the light of Luke 9:57, 58.

10 Luke Chapter 10

We are used to thinking of Jesus having just twelve followers. Yet this chapter teaches us that at this time there were seventy more who were sufficiently strong in spiritual understanding to go out in the Lord's name.

The seventy sent out (10:1-12)

As with the sending of the twelve (9:1-6), the Lord directed them to take very little with them. They were to rely solely on the provision of God. This group was sent to prepare the way for the Messiah, before he arrived at cities and villages. This perhaps meant that the seventy did not have to be so well versed in the truth as the twelve, who operated their campaign without the direct assistance of Jesus.

Christ says, 'The harvest truly is great, but the labourers are few' (v. 2). Indeed at that time the people of Israel had what seems to have been a great hunger for the word of God. The Pharisees had sunk into traditionalism, the Sadducees into error, and the people needed to hear the pure word of God.

Jesus invited those who were already labouring—the seventy—to pray for more workers (v. 2). Too often we divide the church into those who are active in serving the Lord and those who pray for them. The active must pray also. Too often a ministry or mission has been defeated, not by laziness, but prayerlessness. The seventy were to heal the sick, and tell the people that 'the kingdom of God has come near to you' (vv. 9, 11). In many ways, Christ personally represented this kingdom (see comments on Luke 9:27).

As in the case of the twelve disciples, there would be judgement where the message was not received. It is a most solemn and serious thing for the gospel to be rejected (vv. 10-12).

The judgement of God (10:13-16)

In a sense this section begins at verse 10. The Lord anticipated the fact that some cities would reject the truth. He then launched an attack upon Chorazin, Bethsaida and Capernaum, three Galilean towns well known to him. Chorazin stood just two miles from Capernaum by the Sea of Galilee. Bethsaida was the scene of the feeding of the five thousand (Luke 9:10ff). Capernaum was at one time called the Lord's own city (Matt. 9:1). Many miracles were performed there, including the healing of the paralysed man.

Jesus was familiar with the inhabitants of these towns, and their resistant ways. He reminded the people of how blessed these towns had been—mighty works had been done here, works that would have moved even pagans to repentance. The Lord compared these towns to Tyre and Sidon, whose inhabitants were fiercely rebuked by the Lord in the Old Testament.

The people of Capernaum had a sense of their own spiritual importance, and boasted a beautiful synagogue. Jesus had spent a great deal of time there. Yet, though 'exalted to heaven' with many blessings, they would be 'brought down to Hades' (v. 15). As Christ taught on another occasion, 'everyone to whom much is given, from him much will be required' (Luke 12:48).

Joy as the seventy return (10:17-24)

The preaching and healing campaign of the seventy was at an end. They returned with joy and declared that in the all-prevailing name of Jesus, even demons obeyed them. The Lord encouraged them by saying four things:

SATAN IS DEFEATED. The antidote to darkness is light. If only there would be less complaining about the evils in the world, and more done to conquer Satan's kingdom!

AUTHORITY IS GIVEN. He gave them authority over snakes, scorpions and 'all the power of the enemy'. This task would be just the beginning of great work done in the Master's name (see Mark 16:16; Rom. 16:20).

PROTECTION IS PROMISED. 'Nothing shall by any means hurt you' (v. 19). His protection would be a great stimulus to service.

ASSURANCE IS GRANTED. The great cause for rejoicing should not be wonderful works, as these could be performed even by those who are far from Christ (Matt. 7:22, 23) but the fact of being truly saved. To have our names written in heaven is the greatest blessing we can have.

Jesus further rejoices in the revelation of the truth and it is noteworthy that the Lord gave the seventy no cause for pride or self-congratulation, making it clear here that this revelation was given to those who were ignorant children (v. 21).

He proceeded to declare that he could not be known unless he revealed himself to sinners (v. 22). The seventy were privileged to have Christ revealed to them, and to live at the time when wonderful works were done by him, thus his words, 'Blessed are the eyes which see what you see'. Many prophets and kings had desired to see them and could not.

This is very significant in our understanding of the contact between those alive on earth and those in heaven. If ever there was a time when a window upon earth might have been opened in heaven, it was during our Lord's ministry. Clearly the saints in glory cannot see and hear events here below (see Isa. 63:16).

FOR FURTHER STUDY

1. Some have pointed out that the Lord's ministry was intended to mirror in every aspect the Old Testament Scriptures, which he came to fulfil. He chose twelve disciples, just as there were twelve tribes of Israel, and sent out seventy disciples, just as there were seventy elders in the days of Moses (Num. 11:16).

2. See Luke 10:13, 14. God rebuked Tyre in Ezekiel 26-28 for rejoicing when Jerusalem was overthrown (see Ezek. 26:2) and Sidon for their animosity towards his people (Ezek. 28:20-24). Had Tyre and Sidon seen the 'mighty works' done in the towns of Galilee, they would have repented (v. 13). How far does God assess not only our past actions, but also what we might have done under given circumstances? (Compare Luke 11:32 and Matt. 23:29-31.)

3. Some people would like to see their name in lights (Luke 10:20). Yet read where it is most important to have our names: Isaiah 49:16; Revelation 20:12-15.

4. How far was truth concealed from the disciples? See Luke 10:21 and 18:24.

TO THINK ABOUT AND DISCUSS

1. The seventy prepared the way for the Lord himself. How far can any believer be said to be a co-worker with Christ (2 Cor. 6:1)?
2. Christ told the seventy to eat and drink what was set before them (vv. 7, 8). Are we too fussy about what we eat and drink? Is this a bad witness?
3. Are we too casual when people reject the gospel today (Luke 10:10-16)? Should we say more to impress upon men and women their danger if they refuse Christ?
4. What are the spiritual blessings that your community has enjoyed in the past? Are the people in as great danger as Chorazin or Capernaum if they reject the truth?
5. How important is the name of Christ in all we do? (See Acts 3:16; 4:18.)
6. Consider Luke 10:23, 24. Why is it foolish to try to contact the dead?

The Good Samaritan (10:25-37)

This parable follows a conversation Jesus had with a teacher of the Law of Moses, or 'lawyer'. They spoke together about eternal life, and the Lord directed him to the law. It must be remembered that 'the law is spiritual' (Rom. 7:14) and therefore in no way takes us away from eternal life. Instead it exposes our sin and ultimately leads us to see our need of Christ (Gal. 3:24).

Sometimes the words of verse 27 (from Deut. 6:5 and Lev. 19:18) can trip off the tongue; yet do we really love God and our neighbour to the extent Christ intended? The lawyer desired to 'justify himself' (v. 29)—that is, he wanted to appear righteous.

The parable which follows is found only in Luke, yet is so familiar to us today that something of its impact can be lost.

Jesus wanted people to identify with the wounded man, and so described a man who almost certainly was a Jew, undertaking a journey familiar to his hearers. It was a dangerous and solitary path, and the loneliness of this route can still be experienced by the modern traveller.

The man was set upon by thieves who left him in a terrible state, half-dead on the ground. Then two 'religious' Jews walked past. Here we feel the timeless quality of this parable, since people in all ages have walked past the needy lying in the road. Fear, embarrassment, helplessness all conspire to make people pass by. No doubt the priest and the Levite were in a hurry to do God's work, yet they neglected the heart of the law—love for God and for one's neighbour!

The Lord then, with great skill, cast a Samaritan in the role of heroic stranger. The Jews were no friends with the Samaritans, and regarded them almost on a level with demons (John 8:48). For a Samaritan to befriend the wounded man would have seemed unthinkable. Yet Christ's kingdom would ultimately cross all boundaries of race, culture and class. The Samaritan, though apparently alone and unseen by others, showed great kindness. Too often, we are kind to others because we expect recognition and praise for it. The Samaritan could so easily have walked past, and let the man die. No one would have known, and therefore no one would have censured him. But he could not ignore the need.

He first 'had compassion' then bandaged the man's wounds, pouring in oil and wine; the oil to soothe and heal and the wine to cleanse the wound. Next he put the man on his own animal and took him to an inn to care for him. The man paid money (equivalent to two days' wages) to the innkeeper, and offered to pay as much as necessary for the man to recover fully.

The Samaritan had been the true neighbour. The answer to our Lord's question was clear (v. 36) and his intention for his listeners was also unmistakeable: 'Go and do likewise'.

Mary and Martha (10:38-42)

The Lord frequently stayed with Mary, Martha and their brother Lazarus at Bethany, near to Jerusalem. Here were disciples who had not become homeless in following the Lord, but who used and opened their home for him.

Mary sat at his feet and listened attentively as he spoke. Martha, her sister, was busy preparing food for everyone. Martha asked him to rebuke Mary because she needed her help. Yet to have left so noble a guest on his own would have been rude and foolish. Mary used her time wisely, and was nourished by the word of God, infinitely more important food than could be served on a plate (Luke 4:4).

Like the parable of the Good Samaritan, this small account is timeless. We all have aspects of Mary and Martha within us. Perhaps our modern, active church life more closely resembles that of Martha than Mary. We tend to be 'distracted with much serving' today, and only rarely spend time sitting at our Lord's feet and hearing his word.

FOR FURTHER STUDY

1. The Jewish people generally despised the Samaritans because their ancestors were Jews who had intermarried with the enemies of the Jewish people, the Assyrians. Their beliefs became an evil mixture of idolatry and truth, sometimes called syncretism. For the biblical account, see 2 Kings 17:22-41.

2. Luke 17:15-19 and John 4:7-10 help us to see the Samaritans as people, not enemies. Today, in our culture, whom might we regard as our enemies? Is it hard to love them?

3. Consider Luke 10:38-42. The Bible emphasizes the importance of devotion and activity. Isaiah 40:31 suggests that waiting on God gives strength to act. In Luke 10:2 the active labourers were to pray for more people to join in the harvest. In Exodus 17:9-11, Moses prayed as Joshua fought. How can we achieve the right balance?

4. 'Lord, do you not care…?'(v. 40). How often is this cry heard in Scripture? See, for instance, Psalm 10:1; and Mark 4:38. Do we say this today?

TO THINK ABOUT AND DISCUSS

1. The 'Good Samaritan' stopped to help a man he did not know. How should a Christian help in the following instances: A wounded man who is obviously drunk; a person trying to push-start his car (could we apply Deut. 22:4 here?); two people who are quarrelling or fighting in the street?

2. No doubt the priest and the Levite were in a hurry to serve God. Have we struck the right balance between our devotion to God and kindness to our neighbour?

3. Would it be right to be late for church if we have helped someone? Would it ever be wrong to be late for church? Mention some real-life situations.

4. Today, at meals and social gatherings, is it wrong to be discussing spiritual things when others are working hard to serve us? How does Mary's example guide us?

5. If you are like Martha, are you a victim of your circumstances?

11 Luke Chapter 11

On this occasion, Jesus was seen to pray. It may be that something of the reality of his communication with the Father stirred up the disciples to ask for advice on prayer. They knew that John had guided his followers on this subject.

'Teach us to pray' (11:1-4)

Christ could have refused to answer this request, and simply commented that prayer is a spiritual matter requiring no forethought at all. Yet the Lord was well aware of how self-centred and aimless prayer can be sometimes. If we really believe that we are speaking to the sovereign Lord of the universe—who spoke and worlds were created—then our prayers will be more God-centred and purposeful.

He seems to have intended by these few words of instruction to guide disciples as to what themes should be central to prayer.

'OUR FATHER IN HEAVEN,

HALLOWED BE YOUR NAME'

These opening words focus our gaze upon God. We are not approaching him casually; we are not going to begin with self, but with him. Nor are we going to take his name in vain by endless repetitions of 'dear Lord' or 'Gracious God'. His name is holy.

'YOUR KINGDOM COME.
YOUR WILL BE DONE
ON EARTH AS IT IS IN HEAVEN.'

The Lord continued with two petitions that focus on God's rule. The first relates to the kingdom of God. Disciples of Christ are to long for the day when he shall return, and everything shall be under his feet (1 Cor. 15:24-26). The next is that God's will be done 'on earth as it is in heaven'. Submission to God, and delight in his will are vital to true prayer. Too often today, we mistrust God, and find it difficult to submit totally to him (see comments on Luke 5:12).

'GIVE US DAY BY DAY OUR DAILY BREAD.
AND FORGIVE US OUR SINS,
FOR WE ALSO FORGIVE EVERYONE WHO IS INDEBTED TO US.'

Only now are we permitted in this prayer to consider ourselves and our own needs. How simple these petitions seem to be! We need nourishment for the body and forgiveness for the soul. There is no encouragement to ask for luxuries, but only for the necessities of the body. How strange it must seem to God to hear people praying to him all over the world, some for a bowl of rice and others for a brand new sports car!

Christ did not want us to focus on ourselves for the rest of the prayer. Considering forgiveness means we have to think of those who have offended us, and be sure to have cleared them of their 'debt' to us. Luke is the only Gospel writer who records the expression 'debts' rather than 'trespasses'. Luke's account of this prayer is the shortest. We can deduce by the flexibility of expression that the Lord Jesus in no way intended this prayer to be uttered thoughtlessly as just another empty repetition!

'AND DO NOT LEAD US INTO TEMPTATION,

BUT DELIVER US FROM THE EVIL ONE.'

This petition ends the prayer. We pray not only to be kept from outward sin, but even from the inclination to sin. The *desire* to do wrong is still failure in the sight of God. In this petition Christ reveals to us the very close link between the work of 'the evil one' (Satan) and temptation to sin, just as in the Garden of Eden. How we need to pray each day for strength to resist the devil!

We need to be constantly on our guard, to 'watch and pray' against temptation (Mark 14:38). Yet the great example of one who was victorious over every assault of the devil is the Lord Jesus Christ. He is our great High Priest. He sympathizes with our trials and faults for he was tempted in every conceivable way, yet lived without sin. His glorious example should encourage us to resist evil (Heb. 2:18, 4:15).

FOR FURTHER STUDY

1. The Lord's prayer certainly was not intended to be repeated thoughtlessly, as the context of Matthew 6:7-9 illustrates. There we see that prayer was never to be a 'vain repetition'.

2. 'Forgive us our sins, for we also forgive everyone who is indebted to us' (v. 4). Mark

11:25, 26 shows the importance of forgiveness even as we 'stand praying'. Why can't we be devoted to God alone, regardless of how we feel about people? Consider this in the light of 1 John 4:20.

3. We have to forgive up to 'seven times' in a day (Luke 17:3, 4). Yet this number is not a limitation as the sequel so clearly shows! (See Matt. 18:21, 22.)

4. Look at Luke11:4. James tells us we are never tempted by God, but by our own evil desires (James 1:13, 14). Alongside the gunpowder of our own susceptibility is the fire of Satan, to encourage actual sin. Satan is called 'the Tempter'—(See 1 Cor. 7:5; 10:13; 1 Thes. 3:5).

5. Refer to Luke 11:4. David asked God for strength to resist temptation (see Ps. 141:3, 4). Yet we find him weak on the day he saw Bathsheba (2 Sam. 11:1-4). How far must we be balanced in asking God for help and keeping ourselves pure (1 Tim. 5:22)?

TO THINK ABOUT AND DISCUSS

1. Look again at Luke 11:2. Are our prayers sufficiently 'God-centred'? Where does the focus of our prayers tend to be today, and in our particular congregation?

2. Should the general form of the Lord's prayer be a guide to all prayer?

3. Luke 11:3 suggests we are not encouraged to ask for luxuries or expensive meals. Would simpler meals and plainer living be better for us?

4. 'Hallowed be your name'. When does 'Lord' or 'God' become an empty repetition in one's speech?

5. Consider Luke 11:4. In what circumstances might we say that God forgives us on condition that we forgive others?

Principles of prayer (11:5-13)

Jesus gave examples from ordinary human experience to teach the importance of prayer. The first example is of a man calling on a friend at midnight. The man disturbed his friend, asking for bread. In New Testament times, families slept in the same bed for warmth. The man at first refused to give assistance in case he woke the family. The Lord pointed out that eventually the man got up and helped his friend—not because it was a man he knew so well but simply because of the friend's persistence. So in prayer, God is familiar with us and our needs, yet a persistent intercessor will receive many blessings.

In Luke 11:9-13, Jesus proceeded to teach us that God can be trusted. He is our heavenly Father and, as such, will not give us anything harmful. A father on earth would not give his son a stone or a scorpion. Here Christ shows us that there is something wonderfully simple about prayer. It is not as complex as we might think; we must simply ask, seek and knock—God will grant our requests according to his will. If we ask for the Holy Spirit, in particular, this blessing will be granted.

In 1886, the missionary Hudson Taylor was setting out to evangelize eleven provinces in China which had never been visited by missionaries before. Of those who feared for him and his family he said,

> 'I am taking my children with me, and I notice that it is not difficult for me to remember that the little ones need breakfast in the morning, dinner at midday, and something before they go to bed at night. Indeed, I could not forget it.

And I find it impossible to suppose that our Heavenly Father is less tender or mindful than I.'

FOR FURTHER STUDY

1. Luke 11:5-8 shows the importance of persistent prayer. The parable of the 'importunate widow' (Luke 18:1-8) teaches much the same principle.
2. The Lord Jesus implies by this parable that God is like a friend (Luke 11:5-8, and see Exod. 33:11a). In Luke 15 he is like a forgiving father. In Luke 18:1-8 he is seen as a judge, though in contrast to the hard-hearted magistrate depicted there, God avenges us speedily. What other aspects of God's character do the teachings of Jesus reveal?
3. In Luke 11:13, Christ promises that God will give the Holy Spirit to those who ask him. In James 1:5, wisdom is promised to those who ask. In Scripture, what other blessings are promised to those who ask for them?

TO THINK ABOUT AND DISCUSS

1. Jesus encouraged persistent prayer (Luke 11:8). Was this because persistence is a measure of how strongly we feel about a matter?
2. Consider Luke 11:9. The apostle Paul asked three times for an affliction to be removed (2 Cor. 12:7-9). Is there ever a point at which we should stop asking for a particular thing?
3. Our Lord's listeners are called 'evil' seemingly almost in passing (Luke 11:13) and in Matthew 6:34 each day is said to have its own share of 'evil'. How far would the daily consideration of these remarks help us?

Casting out demons (11:14-26)

The Lord had just cast out a demon which had made a person mute. The person could speak again, and although the 'multitudes marvelled', some found fault. They said his power must come from Beelzebub, the ruler of demons.[8] Others wanted more, and desired to see a sign from heaven. Christ knew their thoughts and explained that if it were by Beelzebub that demons were driven out, Satan's kingdom would be divided!

> A clean life, without the Spirit of God, makes us susceptible to further attacks. Indeed, when the demon returns with seven spirits more wicked than himself, the final state of the man is deplorable.

Here Jesus was teaching many lessons at once, stressing the importance of unity, and many have applied his words to the church. Also, he was pointing out that other people claimed to have exorcized demons (v. 19). Were they using Beelzebub's power?

The Lord then revealed a little more of his own identity (vv. 21-23). He, the 'stronger man', had stripped Satan of his armour and robbed him of his spoils. Rather than criticize and resist the ministry of Jesus, the people should have bowed before him. 'He who is not with me is against me' (v. 23).

Christ further taught the people that an unclean spirit driven out of a man might one day return. Once set free, the person may 'clean up' his life, and avoid some of his past sin.

Yet here the Saviour was showing that good morals are not enough. A clean life, without the Spirit of God, makes us susceptible to further attacks. Indeed, when the demon returns with seven spirits more wicked than himself, the final state of the man is deplorable. In Matthew 12:45, these words were to be applied not only to individuals, but to a whole generation which relied on good works and clean living to obtain heaven.

FOR FURTHER STUDY

1. See Luke 11:15. The Lord was often misunderstood during his ministry. He was called 'A glutton and a winebibber, a friend of tax collectors and sinners' (Luke 7:34), one who 'misleads the people' (Luke 23:14). People said, 'You are a Samaritan and have a demon' (John 8:48). God's people today must not be surprised when their actions and motives are similarly misunderstood (see Matt. 10:25).
2. People who saw Christ miraculously cast out demons wanted 'a sign from heaven' (v. 16). Look up Mark 15:31, 32. Many people today say they would believe in Jesus if they could see him. Yet it is important to notice that even the crowds who saw the crucified Lord demanded more, that they might 'see and believe'.
3. How significant is the expression 'the finger of God' (v. 20)? See also Exodus 8:19 and 31:18.
4. Jesus clearly defined his terms. 'He who is not with me is against me' (v. 23). The Lord spoke of humanity as divided between 'sheep' and 'goats' (Matt. 25:32, 33). He taught, 'You cannot serve God and mammon' (Luke 16:13). How far should believers see everything as 'black and white'?

TO THINK ABOUT AND DISCUSS

1. The Lord expected those who heard him to use reasoned arguments when they

questioned him. If Satan's kingdom is divided, it falls. If Christ drives out demons with the finger of God, then 'the kingdom of God has come upon you' (v. 20). How can we best use reason in talking about Christ?

2. In the light of Luke 11:17 and John 17:22, 23, how important is church unity?

3. Why is it not good enough for someone's life to be 'swept and put in order'? Do we make it clear to the world today that good morals are not enough?

Correcting opinions (11:27-32)

For many people, Mary the mother of Jesus towers above the rest of humanity, and is worthy of the utmost reverence. Here Jesus dealt such a view a decisive blow. A woman spoke words which many devout people might utter today: 'Blessed is the womb that bore you…' Jesus refused to accept idle praise—if a viewpoint was unhelpful, however well meaning it might be, he rebuked it.

His reply teaches us that we must beware of putting Mary on a pedestal. Holiness is a virtue accessible to all that follow him. You and I can make the choice to serve God in holiness, or to obey our sinful nature. Virtue is not the prerogative of a canonized handful of followers.

Christ could see that the people gathered to see him perform a miracle (vv. 29-32) but he refused to satisfy worldly curiosity. The only sign would be that of Jonah the prophet. What seems quite dark and cryptic (v. 29) is explained more fully in Matthew 12:40. The reference to Jonah relates primarily to the burial of Christ and, in this sense, Jonah prefigured Christ. Here, for those with ears to hear, Jesus predicted his resurrection.

Having compared himself to the prophet Jonah, the Lord then likened himself to Solomon. In many ways this great king was also a type of Christ. During his reign there was peace in Israel. (Solomon means 'peaceful', and the Lord Jesus is the 'Prince of peace'—Isa. 9:6.) The Queen of Sheba, here called the 'Queen of the South', travelled across land and sea to meet Solomon. Yet Jesus is far greater.

Christ returned to speaking about Jonah, pointing out that this prophet rescued over 120,000 people simply by warning the people of Nineveh. Yet the generation that heard Christ himself—one greater than Jonah—remained stubborn in their sins. How foolish and blind they appeared! Luke has already touched upon this in Luke 10:13-16.

In Luke 11:33-36, the Lord described the importance of light as opposed to darkness, primarily addressing our senses. If our eyes are 'bad' (v. 34), our whole body is full of darkness. Yet if our eye is good, our whole body is full of light. If we see not the Lord of glory but just a teacher who should entertain us with signs, we will sink into the gloom of our own prejudice and sin.

Dinner conversation (11:37-54)

To anyone who imagined that dinner with the Lord Jesus consisted of quiet pleasantries, these verses come as a shock. In many homes you will find a small plaque with the inscription 'Christ is the head of this house, the unseen guest at every meal, the *silent* listener to every conversation.' While the sentiment may be good, we should remember that the Pharisees and lawyers would have felt much more comfortable if Jesus had been 'the silent listener to every conversation'!

The first thing the Pharisees noticed was that Jesus had not washed before dinner. They were fastidious about ceremonial washings, and for them such a practice was vital if they were to be clean in the eyes of the Most High. Whatever etiquette might have taught, the Lord intended to expose their hypocrisy and sin.

We find that this simple remark started a torrent of stern rebuke. We must remember that there were others listening to the Lord, as the context shows, and therefore he was not singling out his host, but rebuking Pharisaism as a whole.[9] He told the Pharisees that they were clean outside, 'but your inward part is full of greed and wickedness.' He was not thinking the worst for its own sake; he simply had to tell them the truth about themselves. He continued by saying, 'You are like graves which are not seen'. Under the law of Moses, to walk on a grave would render one ceremonially unclean. Such defilement occured unwittingly when people came near to the Pharisees!

This hardly seems like ordinary mealtime conversation! A lawyer cautiously stated that those, like him, who scrupulously studied the law, were guilty of the same reproach. Perhaps he expected Jesus to confine his criticism to the Pharisees. Instead, the Lord launched a devastating tirade upon them also: 'Woe to you also, lawyers!' (v. 46).

The Lord rebuked them for their wearisome interpretation of the law, binding heavy burdens upon others, although they did not touch them 'with one of [their] fingers'. He also accused them of persecuting God's people, and held them responsible for the blood of Abel to the blood of Zechariah

(v. 51)—that is, the blood of all the persecuted people of God mentioned in the Scriptures up to that time!

The lawyers not only made God's law burdensome, but they actually hindered those who sought spiritual knowledge (v. 52).

The vindictive response of the scribes and the Pharisees (vv. 53, 54) reveals that Jesus had struck raw nerves when he rebuked their hypocrisy. The lawyers seemed to have been more careful in their response. The scribes and Pharisees, however, sought his downfall.

In case we are left with the mistaken notion that Christ was entirely negative here, we must remember that his words were carefully thought out and balanced. For instance, he told them positively to show kindness to the poor (v. 41). He was also careful not to discountenance obedience to the Law, mentioning how they gave a tenth of even the smallest herbs from their gardens (v. 42) and yet passed by 'justice and the love of God', then adding, 'These you ought to have done, *without leaving the others undone.*' There is balance and care here.

FOR FURTHER STUDY

1. See Luke 11:31. At Solomon's coronation, the earth 'split' because of the great shout of joy from the people (1 Kings1:39, 40). Jesus is surely worthy of greater reverence than Solomon, for he himself is 'greater' (11:31). Do we praise him enough?
2. Consider Luke 11:34. The sins of Eve (Gen. 3:6), Achan (Josh. 7:21) and David (2 Sam. 11:1-4) began with their eyes. Consider the following verses in relation to how we use our eyes: Job 31:1; Psalm 119:37 and 2 Peter 2:14.
3. The lawyers (vv. 45-52) were people who devoted their lives to the detailed study of God's law. Yet, it seems, they saw it as a massive rulebook. Are we ever in danger of presenting the gospel in the same way?
4. Look up Luke 11:47-50. To what extent should a generation share in the guilt of those who lived before they were born? (See Deut. 23:3, 4.)

TO THINK ABOUT AND DISCUSS

1. Consider Luke 11:27. How far should we be ready to correct what others say to us, even if they appear well meaning? When should we let a misguided comment pass us by?
2. See Luke 11:37-54. In John Bunyan's *Pilgrim's Progress*, Christian remarks to Faithful, after his firm rebuke of a sinner, 'There is but little of this faithful dealing with men nowadays'. Are we more concerned to be polite than faithful to the truth?
3. The Lord's anger did not make him unreasonable, as we see from verse 42. How can we tell when our anger has gone too far? How does Scripture guide us in this respect?
4. Look at Luke 11:44. Are there people who might contaminate the unwary, like unmarked graves, today?
5. Think about Luke 11:46. In our presentation of the word of God, how might we be in danger of loading men with burdens?

12 Luke Chapter 12

Luke 12 deals forcibly with the importance of living in the light of eternity. It is the Kingdom of God, not material things, which must take first place.

The day of reckoning (12:1-12)

Celebrities naturally resent it when the media digs too deeply into their personal lives. Most of us sympathize with them, and see it as an imposition. We are very fond of our privacy. Yet the Lord Jesus teaches us that what is hidden and whispered about will one day be seen and heard by all. There is no such thing as hiding from the all-seeing eyes of God. The Pharisees were hypocrites in this way—their holiness was renowned and their sins hidden from public gaze. Yet a day of reckoning was approaching.

The Lord told a vast crowd (so great that people began to trample one another) exactly what the Pharisees did not want them to hear, saying, 'Beware of the leaven of the Pharisees' (v. 1). Just as yeast ('leaven') expands the dough and affects a whole loaf of bread, so the contaminating effect of hypocrisy spreads. God's all-seeing eye regards everything we do, and his ear records all we say (v. 3)—therefore we must fear him and prepare to give account to him.

In Luke 12:4-7, the Saviour proceeded by telling this vast crowd not to fear man, but only God. Other people may be able to kill our bodies, but he has 'power to cast into hell' (v. 4, 5). God's power and justice are infinite, and the suffering of hell will far outlast the anger of man.

Too often we disregard this, and only fear people. How often, when we sin, do we feel little or no guilt until someone finds out and confronts us? Then we suddenly start to tremble! Our lives need to be spotless in private as well as in public. Do we really fear the unseen God?

The Lord then teaches us concerning the gentleness and thoughtfulness of God the Father. He is indeed the stern Judge of all the earth, but it must also be remembered that he desires the very best for his people. His laws are not intended to shame or destroy us, but are for our benefit. God has tender care for the smallest detail of our lives. Five sparrows are sold for two copper coins and not one of them is forgotten by God—you are worth more than 'many sparrows'. Even the hairs of our heads are all numbered by God.

Next, our Lord deals with an issue relevant to every age, but especially to his hearers on that day, speaking of the importance of boldly declaring him in the face of fierce opposition. It is difficult to be willing to endure mockery or even death for the sake of one whom we cannot see. The writer to the Hebrews tells us that this was the grand secret of Moses' spiritual walk with God: 'he endured as seeing him who is invisible' (Heb. 11:27). It was this which helped Daniel's three friends prefer to be thrown into a furnace than deny the true and living God (Dan. 3).

The Lord adds that blasphemy against the Holy Spirit cannot be forgiven. Here again, he speaks about the Day of Judgement. Everyone must be warned about that great day when all secret things are disclosed. People may mock us for confessing Christ, but they must be severely warned about careless and blasphemous words against the Holy Spirit. We must always address God with the deepest reverence.

The same Holy Spirit will help God's people to speak when they are brought before 'magistrates and authorities' (vv. 11, 12). We can see the literal fulfilment of these words as we read the Acts of the Apostles. Where did Peter, Stephen and Paul get their wisdom and power when they spoke of Christ to the authorities? It was from the Holy Spirit himself.

God has plans too: the parable of the rich fool (12:13-21)

This parable is in context of shunning materialism. From the crowd, a man asked Jesus to be the arbiter, and divide an estate between two brothers. This was an unusual request, but we can understand a man asking himself, 'Who better to be fair and just than the Lord Jesus?' Interestingly, he refuses to get involved.

In the parable itself, we can detect a timeless theme—the love of this world. The Saviour spoke of a man who would have considered himself blessed. His fields yielded plentiful crops, too bulky to be stored in his barns. The wealthy farmer did not seem unduly fretful at the prospect of rebuilding his barns, or expanding his business. Most of us might have admired him as a capable businessman. Perhaps some of our Lord's hearers would feel envy at the cosy nature of this man's promise to himself (v. 19). Isn't this exactly the kind of material prosperity—carefree living for many years—that we all want?

But God called the man a fool. That very night he died, and all his wealth went to another. Christ tells us that all who lay up treasure for themselves, and are not 'rich toward God', are fools. Where do you stand?

FOR FURTHER STUDY

1. Look again at Luke 12:3. Achan, Gehazi, Ananias and Sapphira, and forty assassins who plotted to kill Paul all found that their secret plans came to light even before the Day of Judgement (see Josh. 7:10-26, 2 Kings 5:20-27, Acts 5:1-11 and Acts 23:11-16). How many secret sins come to light today?
2. Reflect on Luke 12:7. Here we see that God is concerned not only about the great and important things of this world, but that he cares also for the smallest details of our existence. The average person has over 100,000 hairs on his or her head, but only God knows the exact number!
3. See Luke 12:7 and compare Luke 21:12-19, which speaks of the certainty of future persecution for believers. What kind of protection is our Lord Jesus speaking of in Luke 21:18?
4. Consider Luke 12:13, 14. To what extent can we apply Paul's teaching in 2 Timothy 2:3, 4 to our Lord's response here?
5. See Luke 12:18, 19 and James 4:13-16. In the light of these scriptures, how often should we make it clear that our plans are made 'God willing'?

TO THINK ABOUT AND DISCUSS

1. Often what is done in secret comes to light and the world discovers a secret weakness about someone. Would we live differently if we seriously considered that all that is said and done in secret will one day be 'proclaimed on the housetops' (v. 3)?
2. Read Luke 12:4-12. Our actions, however hidden from the world, are seen by angels, demons, Satan and the living God. Why is it that we tend to fear God least of all?
3. Consider Luke 12:10. For what reason do you think that the Holy Spirit in particular must never be blasphemed?
4. Think about Luke 12:18, 19. When do our plans and hopes for the future resemble those of the rich fool?

Don't worry (12:22-34)

I used to have a small statue at home of a worried monster. Its plinth read, 'Don't just sit there…Worry!' It was surprising to me how often I found myself looking at this object with a tight brow, worried about this or that. If we kept a record of all the times we are anxious in the course of a week, or even a day, it might surprise us. Worry overshadows our days and freezes our creativity. Worry can be a sin when its origins lie in unbelief and a mistrust of God.

The word 'therefore' (v. 22) implies that the verses which follow are an exposition of the parable of the rich fool. We must consider the ravens, which have 'neither storehouse nor barn' yet God feeds them. We are to 'sell' what we have and give to those in need. In this way we will have 'treasure in the heavens that does not fail, where no thief approaches nor moth destroys' (v. 33). How hard it is to obey our Saviour's teaching! Our possessions and affluent western lifestyle show that few of us take our Lord seriously. He connects wealth to worry. He teaches his disciples to travel light if they would have treasure that cannot be stolen or destroyed. The Son of God calls his people to be totally different from the 'nations' of this world (v. 30).

Christ was not dealing with foolish fears, but very practical concerns. We might call them very necessary worries. He says we must not fret over food or drink (v. 29). If even the necessities of our daily survival should not worry us, how much less concerns about holidays, investments or cars!

FOR FURTHER STUDY

1. Compare Luke 12:22-34 and Matthew 6:24-34. What are the similarities and the differences?
2. Look at Luke 12:31. What does it mean truly to 'seek the kingdom of God'?
3. In Philippians 4:6, 7, what is Paul's antidote to anxiety?
4. Consider Luke 12:33, 34. Examine these words in relation to Psalm 62:10, Proverbs 30:8 and the very similar statement in Proverbs 13:7.

TO THINK ABOUT AND DISCUSS

1. If worrying achieves nothing (v. 25), why are we so fretful?
2. Read Luke 12:29, 30. How far is the modern Christian different from 'the nations of the world'?
3. What clues would demonstrate that a person zealously sought 'first' the kingdom of God (Luke 12:31)?

4. 'The less we have, the less we worry'. Discuss this statement in the light of Luke 12:22-34.

5. Consider Luke 12:33, 34. Paul rejoiced when poor believers in Macedonia gave even beyond their means (2 Cor. 8:1-4). Do we give today in a way that is deeply sacrificial?

Free or faithful? (12:35-48)

This is further exposition of the parable of the rich fool, who left this world without being ready to part from his wealth and stand before God (vv. 13-21). The Lord spoke about what happens to servants when their master is away for a long period. The Lord Jesus anticipates the period between his first coming and the second. What would his servants do? Would impatience and worldliness creep in? Would the church lose her sense of accountability and her readiness to meet her Lord?

Everyone knows what it means for the boss to be away. Most people take advantage of such a time to relax and 'go slow' for a while. After all, no one is closely watching! Yet for the Christian, there should be a continual awareness of God, and an hour by hour anticipation of the Lord's return. The faithful and watchful servant would be served by his master (v. 37), for he lived in constant readiness for his return.

Jesus proceeded to explain that on the Day of Judgement, God will deliver fair punishment to all who disregard him. Those who knew their master's will and did not obey will be beaten with 'many' stripes, and those who did not know will be beaten with 'few'. Thus we see that the more we know of the will of God, the more we will be held accountable for how we have lived.

FOR FURTHER STUDY

1. Christ's return is compared to the visit of a 'thief in the night' for those who are not ready for him (cf vv. 38, 40). For the believer, however, his coming should not be a great surprise. (See 1 Thessalonians 5 and compare verse 2 and verse 4.)
2. To be 'cut in two' and appointed a 'portion with the unbelievers' (v. 46) is a description of hell. What other pictures of future judgement do the Gospels give us? See Luke 12:58, 59, Luke16:23, 24, 28, Matthew 18:34 and Mark 9:43-48.
3. Consider Luke 12:48.The Lord Jesus taught the Pharisees, 'If you were blind, you would have no sin; but now you say, "We see." Therefore your sin remains.' John 9:39-41. Those of us who are most familiar with the Word of God will be held most accountable before him. How should we apply Paul's words in Romans 1:20, 21 and Romans 5:12, 13?

TO THINK ABOUT AND DISCUSS

1. For over two thousand years God has been preparing the church to be ready for the return of Christ. If believers in the first century had known that such a long period would pass before the second coming, would they have been so zealous for Christ?
2. In our Lord's parable, unfaithful servants became violent and drunk (12:45). What are the particular dangers today?
3. How can we apply Luke 12:47, 48 to ourselves and our world today?

A world divided (12:49-53)

The Lord tells us that the effect of obeying his radical demands will be huge. He speaks of sending 'fire' upon the earth. He came to transform lives by the power of his Holy Spirit. Is this not the message of John the Baptist when he said, 'I indeed baptize you with water…but he will baptize you with the Holy Spirit and with fire' (Luke 3:16)?

Additionally the Saviour had a 'baptism' to face, a baptism of suffering. His followers would have to be prepared to meet with a violent reaction even as they proclaimed the wonderful teachings of Christ. For instance, James and John had to prepare to suffer for the cause of Christ (Mark 10:38, 39). The world would be angry and resent the truth (see 1 Cor. 2:14).

The Lord came not to bring peace, but a sword. Have you experienced this in your own family? He said three would be divided against two and two against three (v. 52). Perhaps it shocks us that the effect of our Lord's coming upon families could be destructive. Across the world, there are families torn asunder by the fact that some are saved in the family and

The Lord came not to bring peace, but a sword. Have you experienced this in your own family? He said three would be divided against two and two against three (v. 52). Perhaps it shocks us that the effect of our Lord's coming upon families could be destructive.

others not. We must not misunderstand our Lord's words here. He was not teaching that his followers should disown their blood relations; instead he was merely pointing out that conflict occurs when light and darkness meet. This division can range from mild insults to murder. In many strongly Islamic countries today, a Muslim who becomes a Christian can expect fierce opposition and even death from his or her unbelieving relatives.

Get ready (12:54-59)

The Lord was speaking to people accustomed to reading the sky as a barometer. They were familiar with the signs of an approaching shower or heat wave. Yet when it came to spiritual things, they could not 'discern this time'. Had they known it, the people as a whole would have realized that they lived in the age of the Messiah. This was the last opportunity for the nation of Israel to submit to God before the desolation of the land and the scattering of the people.

They were 'hypocrites' because they wanted to appear religious and discerning, yet they understood more about the weather than they did about spiritual things. How important it is that we have a thorough understanding of the Word of God! This will guard us against spiritual blindness and the inability to recognize the fulfilment of prophecy.

The chapter ends with the Saviour expressing the importance of being at peace with our adversary. If a man is in debt, a humble heart and a willingness to be at peace with a creditor will save him from a debtor's prison. The people should be desiring peace with the Messiah, and should submit to him. Otherwise, on his return, they would have to pay the debt of sin in eternal judgement. He ended with a warning: 'I tell you, you shall not depart from there till you have paid the very last mite' (v. 59).

FOR FURTHER STUDY

1. Look again at Luke 12:54-56. In 1 Chronicles 12:32 there were sons of Issachar who 'had understanding of the times, to know what Israel ought to do'. How far are we able to discern the fulfilment of biblical prophecy and the times in which we live?
2. Consider Luke 12:58, 59. How are we to make our peace with God? (See Ps. 85:8 and Rom. 5:1.)
3. See Luke 12:58, 59. Sin is compared to debt, and hell to a debtor's prison. Consider this in the light of Matthew 18:34, Luke 7:41-48 and 11:4.

TO THINK ABOUT AND DISCUSS

1. 'I came to send fire on the earth' (v. 49). Why is it that so many people think of church as a place of restraint and formality?
2. Look up Luke 12:51-53. How should a young Christian deal with parents who want to restrict his or her church attendance?
3. Consider Luke 12:53.What is the church's role in cases where families are deeply divided because of the faith? Is it to seek unity?
4. Do we daily seek to be at peace with God? Answer this in the light of Luke 12:58.

13 Luke Chapter 13

Whenever there is a catastrophe, whether man-made or a natural disaster, understandably people ask, 'Why?' We know that God rules over the earth and is sovereign (Dan. 4:35), yet we are naturally curious to know *why* suffering has occurred. The Lord Jesus wanted his followers to look at themselves and ask, 'Am I right with God? Have I repented of my sin?' Am I ready to stand before the all-holy God?'

'Repent' (13:1-5)

Here reference was made to news of an atrocity committed by Pontius Pilate. He had slaughtered Galileans who had come in peace to Jerusalem, merely to offer sacrifice to God. Pilate was a man of violence, and quite fearful of any sign of Hebrew unrest. (He became friends with murderous Herod at the time of our Lord's crucifixion—Luke 23:12.) The Lord pointed out that this did not occur because the Galileans were worse sinners than others, but that it was a sign that repentance was needed. So also when the tower in Siloam accidentally collapsed, crushing eighteen people, it was not a sign that these were worse sinners than others, but, rather, a call to repentance.

Be fruitful or be cut down (13:6-9)

Here, Jesus is referring to those who have been blessed yet are fruitless. Like a barren fig tree, no fruit had been found for three years. The landowner was angry and wanted it cut down (13:7).

Some see this parable as referring to the nation of Israel. The keeper is the Lord Jesus, and the landowner God the Father. The keeper intercedes for the tree (see Heb. 7:24, 25), promising to do all he can to make it fruitful. We must ask whether we are fruitful in serving the Lord, or we just 'use up' his gifts to us, remaining barren.

FOR FURTHER STUDY

1. Luke 13:1-5. Interpreting providence can be difficult. Sometimes the righteous are cut off, and taken from the evil to come (Isa. 57:1), at other times the wicked are seen to prosper (Ps. 37:35 and 73:3-7). How can we make sense of such things?
2. Israel is compared to a barren fig tree (vv. 6-9), a brood of young chickens (v. 34) and a disappointing vineyard (Isa. 5:1-6). God did so much for his people, yet they bore little fruit. Are we the same?
3. The fruit of the Holy Spirit is listed in Galatians 5:22, 23. Do we aim to bear this fruit in our lives?
4. Look up Matthew 7:21-23. How far does this principle prove that spiritual *fruit* is more important than spiritual gifts?

TO THINK ABOUT AND DISCUSS

1. Look at Luke 13:1-5. Why must we be careful before we say why we think a catastrophe has occurred?
2. 'Unless you repent' (vv. 3, 5). How do you know when a person's repentance is genuine?
3. Consider Luke 13:7. What are the dangers of allowing fruitless believers to continue as members of a church? How might they be 'using up' resources (v. 7b)?
4. Who is the best judge of our spiritual fruitfulness: our families, our church leaders or ourselves? Would the verdict be the same in each case?

The woman bent double (13:10-17)

Far from avoiding Sabbath-day healing, our Lord seemed to specialize in it! He was teaching in a synagogue on the Sabbath and a woman was there who had a disease which seemed to have a demonic origin. A 'spirit of infirmity' had bent her double for eighteen years. What a terrible trial for her! How much suffering and discomfort she had to endure! Christ drew attention to this fact in verse 16, when he said 'think of it…' However, the day of her release had arrived. Jesus did not ask for her request; he simply set her free from her infirmity. He laid hands on her, and immediately she was made straight and glorified God.

The ruler of the synagogue complained, saying that this miracle should have occurred during the six days permitted for work. Jesus, however, rebuked him as a 'hypocrite'. He would think nothing of having compassion upon an ox or a donkey on the Sabbath—so why not a person?

Kingdom expansion (13:18-21)

The Lord gave two pictures of the expansion of the kingdom of God. The first is the growth from a mustard seed to a tree (vv. 18, 19). Elsewhere Jesus pointed out that the mustard seed is 'the least of all the seeds' (Matt. 13:32). Yet this seed grows into a tree sufficiently large for birds to nest in its branches. So the kingdom expands from something almost invisible into a worldwide family.

Similarly the kingdom is like 'leaven' or yeast, which a woman hid in three measures of meal. The yeast caused the entire quantity of meal to rise.

Christianity expanded throughout the Mediterranean region during the first century. The name of Christ was known in Spain, Italy, Asia Minor, Greece, Israel and later Armenia. It grew from twelve disciples to millions of adherents within a century. We can therefore understand our Lord's point about the remarkable growth of the kingdom!

FOR FURTHER STUDY

1. Sometimes the Lord asked the sufferer what he or she wanted before performing a work of healing (Mark 10:51). At other times he healed without asking (e.g. Luke 7:11-15). Why do you think there are these different approaches?

2. Luke 13:20, 21. This is a unique usage of 'leaven' since usually in Scripture it is used as an emblem of evil (see Luke 12:1; 1 Cor. 5:1, 4-7).

TO THINK ABOUT AND DISCUSS

1. A 'spirit of infirmity' was the cause of this disease. How far do you think we can legitimately blame Satan for illness?
2. Do we 'glorify God' (v. 13) whenever we recover from an illness?
3. In what ways and places can we see God's kingdom expanding today?

The narrow way (13:22-30)

At this point in our Lord's journeys throughout Israel, there was a sudden turning toward Jerusalem (v. 22). He 'steadfastly set his face' (Luke 9:51) toward the place of his suffering. From the crowd, one asked him, 'Lord, are there few who are saved?' (v. 23). The Lord had spoken of the kingdom expanding, and perhaps this man overheard people declaring that this would become a worldwide kingdom. Whoever this man was, we know that he wanted some indication of the size of the kingdom. How many would really be saved?

Jesus did not answer this question directly. He had the capability of exactly stating how many people would come to salvation, but he wanted this man to ask, 'Am *I* saved?' Sometimes we concern ourselves over the spiritual progress of other people and yet forget to make sure we enter the kingdom ourselves. Jesus answered by speaking to all who were assembled, 'Strive to enter through the narrow gate'(v. 24). The word 'strive' in the original Greek language lies at the root of our English word 'agonize'—we are to do all we can to squeeze through that narrow gate of repentance and faith.

The Lord immediately declared that one day many would want to enter, but it would be too late. They would then 'seek to enter' and plead the fact that they 'ate and drank' in his presence. They would clutch at straws, boasting that he had taught in their streets. Yet these most solemn words were to be spoken by the Lord: 'Depart from me, all you workers of iniquity' (v. 27).

> The mustard seed will grow; the leaven will affect the whole earth; yet we must ask ourselves, 'Are we part of that kingdom? Have we entered by the strait gate?'

What our Lord said must have filled the mind of every religious Jew with disquiet. There will be a throng 'from the east and the west, from the north and the south' (v. 29) who will enjoy the kingdom of God. These will mostly comprise Gentiles, as what Jesus calls 'the times of the Gentiles' (Luke 21:24) are ushered in (Rom. chapters 10 and 11). The Saviour implies that many of the Jewish people themselves will be 'thrust out' (v. 28). How can this be? John 15:23 stresses that to reject the Lord Jesus is to reject the Father also.

The mustard seed will grow; the leaven will affect the whole earth; yet we must ask ourselves, 'Are we part of that kingdom? Have we entered by the narrow gate?'

Darkening clouds (13:31-35)

How could the kingdom expand in this way if its leader was a fugitive? With mock concern, the Pharisees warned Christ to leave 'for Herod wants to kill you'. How did our Lord react to this threat? He seemed unperturbed, and instead sent the messengers back to 'that fox', Herod, saying that he had to continue the work to which he had been called. On the third day he would be 'perfected' (v. 32)—that is, he would reach his goal, a reference to his completed sacrifice on the cross.

Ironically, he pointed out that 'it cannot be that a prophet perish outside of Jerusalem' (v. 33). A true servant of the living God must perish in the holy city! How had Jerusalem fallen, that had once been the centre of truth for this entire planet! Far from continuing in an ironic tone, however, the Lord lamented the future doom of the city. Truly he felt great compassion for its inhabitants. Later, he would weep over its future (Luke 19:41, 42). As a mother hen, he would have loved to gather its citizens under his wings, but time had run out. 'Your house is left to you desolate' (v. 35).

The Lord ended by saying that the next time they saw him they would recognize his true identity. It may be that he referred here not to his triumphal entry into Jerusalem on Palm Sunday, but to the day he would return in the clouds of heaven as judge of all the earth. On that day the people would use the words of Psalm 118:26 and cry, 'Blessed is he who comes in the name of the LORD'.

FOR FURTHER STUDY

1. Refer to Luke 13:29. The word 'sit' is literally 'recline' in the kingdom of God. Note the contrast between the restlessness of hell and the perfect rest of heaven in Revelation 14:11, 13.
2. 'A Gentile who sought to enter God's kingdom in Old Testament times had hundreds of regulations to follow. Now it's as easy as "Yes, I believe!"' Is this statement true in the light of Luke 13:24?

TO THINK ABOUT AND DISCUS

1. Read Luke 13:23, 24. What idle questions should be turned into practical directives today?
2. What would be the characteristics of a man or woman who 'strives' to enter the narrow gate (v. 24)? Do you know anyone like this, and, if so, how would you advise such a person?
3. Consider Luke 13:24. Is the way to heaven narrower than we think?
4. The people sought to intimidate Jesus. How far should all believers be calm in the face of threats? (See Dan. 3:13-18 and 2 Tim. 1:7.)

14 Luke Chapter 14

Just about the whole section from Luke 14:1 to 18:14 is found only in this Gospel. Here are vivid insights into the core of Christ's teaching concerning the kingdom of heaven, the way of salvation, forgiveness and practical holiness. How we should thank the Lord for the preservation of these truths in Luke's account.

A Sabbath healing (14:1-6)

How hard it must have been for the Son of God to find a moment to relax! Even being invited for a meal was a time to test him out! A ruler of the Pharisees had invited him to have a Sabbath meal. We are told here of something that must have been true many times during his ministry: 'They watched him closely' (v. 1). There was a man present who had dropsy, a disease that involves an accumulation of excess fluid in a body cavity or in the tissues, and is usually accompanied by painful swelling.

Jesus asked them if it was lawful to heal on the Sabbath. It seems, as we have seen time and again, that the Lord especially chose the Sabbath day to heal, and thereby demonstrated the true meaning of that day. He then healed the man and let him go. No one argued with him openly, but he appealed to their concern for animals. 'Which of you, having a donkey or an ox that has fallen into a pit, will not immediately pull him out on the Sabbath day?' (v. 5). Here the Lord used common sense and ordinary compassion to show that what he had done perfectly fulfilled the law, the heart of which is mercy (see Hos. 6:6).

Take the lowest place (14:7-14)

Christ had been invited by a ruler of the Pharisees to a Sabbath dinner and he used the occasion to teach two great truths.

The first concerns humility. He 'noted' how everyone chose for themselves the best places at the table (v. 7). He taught them to make a point in future of choosing the lowest place. This would have a dual effect—firstly, one would avoid embarrassment in case a more important person had to take one's seat, and, secondly, it taught a divine principle: 'Whoever exalts himself will be humbled, and he who humbles himself will be exalted' (v. 11). Jesus told them that if they were to sit in the lowest place, and were called to go higher, people would appreciate them (v. 10).

The second lesson (vv. 12-14) was the importance of showing kindness to those who cannot repay us. We all know the joy of inviting others to dinner and, in return, being invited to their home—the pattern is cosy and fair. How rare it is, however, to throw a dinner party for those who might desperately need the food! Jesus emphasized the importance of inviting those who cannot do the same for us. Jesus desired for us to seek our reward from God alone and not from men (v. 14).

Guess who's coming to dinner? (14:15-24)

One of the people at the table felt a great sense of joy as our Lord spoke of the future reward of the just. He called out, 'Blessed is he who shall eat bread in the kingdom of God!' (v. 15). Again, Jesus used his surroundings as an illustration, in the form of a parable, for another lesson about food. The gospel message is for those who most feel their hunger for the truth, not necessarily those who were first invited.

In this parable there was nothing wrong with the supper—only with the invited guests. The invitation to enjoy this meal went out to all, but they made lame excuses. So it is with the gospel today. I recall a tract which showed a child on the front cover and the caption, 'Too Young…' The next pictures showed people at various stages of life and the captions, 'Too busy to bother…Too old…Too late!' The last picture was of a coffin. People today make excuses as to why they cannot follow Christ—but before they know it, life has passed them by and the doors into the kingdom are shut.

The master was angry when his servant returned and he discovered that his invitations had been snubbed. Immediately he sent the invitation to those who really needed the food. They would be found in 'the streets and lanes of the city' and later in 'the highways and hedges'. They would be compelled to come in, so that the house would be filled with guests.

The parable ends with a note that reflects the seriousness

of its message: 'I say to you that none of those men who were invited shall taste my supper.'

FOR FURTHER STUDY

1. 'They watched him closely' (v. 1). The Babylonian officials likewise watched Daniel (Dan. 6:4). How would our lives and characters stand such a test?
2. The 'prosperity gospel' teaches that Christians should expect material wealth in return for obedience to God. How should we respond to this view in the light of Luke 14:11?
3. The Lord Jesus sometimes spoke of rewards here on earth (Mark 10:29-31) yet ultimately wanted his followers to seek their main reward in the future—Luke 14:14; 6:19-21; 12:33, 34. Why?
4. Luke 14:15-24. How far can it be said that possessions and even marriage can take a man's heart away from a desire for spiritual things (see Luke 16:13; 1 Cor. 7:32-35)?
5. See Luke 14:21, 23. Do the Scriptures encourage us to expect the poor to receive the truth more readily than the rich? (See Luke 6:20; Mark 12:37b.) How far might this principle vary between cultures?

TO THINK ABOUT AND DISCUSS

1. The Son of God often appealed to reason and a sense of the practical (14:5; 6:32, 33). How should we answer those who say his laws are unreasonable or impractical?
2. If believers are special in the eyes of God, why does he desire that they should take the lowest place at meals (v. 10)?
3. How could believers (individually or as churches) best fulfil Luke 14:13 without seeming to be patronizing?
4. Why do people make excuses rather than entering the kingdom of God? Is it that they haven't understood what's on offer, or that they have no relish for it?

The cost of discipleship (14:25-35)

Contrary to popular belief, the Lord Jesus was not desperate to have a large following regardless of the depth of the people's commitment. A great crowd was following him (v. 25)—some leaders would have relished such fame, and tried to teach a popular message to attract some more—yet he said, 'If anyone comes to me and does not hate…' (v. 26). Rather than compromise the truth, he was willing to see the crowd thin out.

He taught about 'hating' our families, by which he meant that the effect of truly following him would be that we seem to hate our own families in the light of the higher priority of allegiance to Christ. Individual believers throughout history have had to reject their family's values and even surrender their inheritance. We must hate our own lives also. This was no attempt at cheap fame or gaining an easy following. Our Lord desired to be plain and truthful and for those who heard him to be under no illusions about the kingdom of God; he taught that we have to sit down and count the cost—just as a builder wanting to construct a tower must check he has enough materials. The desire to build the tower is not enough. We cannot enter Christ's kingdom by our desires alone, but by the practical outworking of faith.

Contrary to popular belief, the Lord Jesus was not desperate to have a large following regardless of the depth of the people's commitment.

He compared it also to a king who is outnumbered two to one. We need to count the cost before telling the world that we are ready to follow Jesus. A sad feature of today's society is that people want instant joy and comfort, without being willing to endure discomfort of any kind. Christ wanted people to deliberate and consider the high level of commitment he requires of them.

Then Christ said something quite astounding in a verse which shines with the lustre of heaven even as it closes for ever our hopes of glories here on earth. 'So likewise, whoever of you does not forsake all that he has cannot be my disciple' (v. 33). This may be more literally translated, 'Whoever does not take leave of all that he himself possesses cannot be my disciple.' Most commentators say that this forsaking of possessions means simply giving up our own control over them. Yet for the first followers of our Saviour these words were taken literally. Their discarded fishing nets bore witness to the high cost of discipleship.

The chapter concludes with our Lord's comparison of believers with salt. Disciples are the salt or 'flavour' of the earth. If they begin to serve Christ, but later shrink back, they become worthless. This is why counting the cost is so important. We must pray for grace to endure to the end in zeal and self sacrifice.

FOR FURTHER STUDY

1. How far is the depth of New Testament commitment to God greater than in Old Testament times?
2. Refer to Luke 14:26. When does 'hate' mean to 'love less?' (Consider carefully Gen. 29:30, 31 and Deut. 21:15.)
3. Consider Luke 14:27. How far should even faithful and spiritual people expect hardship? (See 1 Cor. 4:10-13 and Heb. 11:36-38.)

TO THINK ABOUT AND DISCUSS

1. Look again at Luke 14:26. In what ways might modern believers need to be prepared to upset their families?
2. 'My husband (or wife) is my life.' To what extent should Christians guard against such attitudes?
3. Consider Luke 14:26b. What would be the distinctive features of a Christian who 'hated' his own life?
4. Read Luke14:33 again. When it comes to our attitude to possessions, how far are we dishonest with ourselves?

15 Luke Chapter 15

This chapter is quite unique in the Gospel of Luke. There are three separate parables which essentially illustrate the same message: The Son of God has come to seek and to save the lost.

The Lost Sheep (15:1-7)

Here, at the outset of the chapter, tax collectors, who were regarded as swindlers (see notes on Luke 3:12), and other sinners had drawn near to the Lord to hear him. The Pharisees and scribes complained, saying, 'This man receives sinners and eats with them.' It may seem strange, but throughout history 'religious' people have been tempted to look down on those who most needed their help. Christ replied in a way which would have caught them off guard—time and again the Saviour appealed to human compassion towards animals to illustrate the compassion we need toward people!

The Lord did not speak of the shepherd as unusually kind or thoughtful. Instead Jesus *assumed* the self-sacrificing actions of the shepherd (v. 4). To lose just one sheep may seem in itself no great tragedy; one per cent loss is very small. Why not just accept it? Yet it is clear that the shepherd grieves over the plight of even one lost sheep.

The sheep would not have been left 'in the wilderness' to wander; but would probably have been penned up. Yet their safety was in numbers; whereas the sheep on its own was vulnerable to any predator.

Christ continued by speaking of the joy when the shepherd found the lost sheep: 'he lays it on his shoulders, rejoicing.' Later, he would call friends and neighbours to rejoice with him. In the last verse the Lord delivered a blessing and a blow: 'I say to you that likewise there will be more joy in heaven over one sinner who repents than over ninety-nine just persons who need no repentance' (v. 7). (See notes on Luke 5:31, 32.)

It is a beautiful picture of joy as the sheep is restored. How this picture should encourage sinners to trust the greatest Shepherd! What joy there is in being found! There is nothing here of a reluctant shepherd scolding the sheep, but rather of relief and elation.

The Lost Coin (15:8-10)

Keeping cash at home is not something we encourage in a society based upon the gathering of interest upon capital, where inflation can be unpredictable and where stealing is rife. However, in New Testament times, to keep family treasures (or to bury them) was commonplace. Here a woman had ten silver coins. Sometimes these were worn around the head by women on their wedding day. Each coin represented a day's wages.[10]

This woman lost one, lighted a lamp and swept the house.

All of us have had this experience at one time or another. We know the frantic search for a bunch of keys or perhaps for a passport—the feeling of helplessness, the almost infantile cry as we turn over cushions and books. Jesus knows human nature and understands such moments. Then he describes the relief on finding the coin—the joy as friends and neighbours are called to share in the happiness of this time.

It seems the Lord wanted hard-hearted and foolish sinners to consider the depth of his longing for our restoration, and his great joy when we are at last restored to him.

FOR FURTHER STUDY

1. How far does the thought of Christ as our Shepherd comfort us? (See Ps. 23:1; John 10:11-15.)
2. How far are we all like wandering sheep before conversion…and perhaps afterwards? (See Ps. 119:17; Isa. 53:6; Mark 6:34; 1 Peter 2:25.)
3. Look up Psalm 38:5 and Isaiah 53:6. How far can we say that wandering from God is foolish and hurtful to ourselves?

TO THINK ABOUT AND DISCUSS

1. Why is it that so often people are naturally compassionate toward animals, yet have to work hard to be merciful to other people? (See Luke 14:5, 6 and Prov. 12:10.)
2. How zealous should a church be to restore a backslider? What are the best ways of approaching such a person? What should we not do?
3. Explain why it is so dangerous for a person to wander away from regular Christian fellowship.
4. Should we take time to really rejoice with our friends when God brings us out of a trial (see Luke 15:6, 9, 22, 23)?

The Lost Son (15:11-32)

This final example of loss and restoration is perhaps the most poignant. Here Jesus expressed most vividly the foolishness of sin and the faithfulness of God. The parable begins with a man, probably very wealthy, and his two sons. It is his younger son who wanted to leave home. He asked for his inheritance money ahead of the death of his father. In ancient times it was not unknown for sons to receive their inheritance while their father was still alive. Indeed this is how Abraham treated his son Isaac, giving also smaller gifts to his other children (Gen. 25:5, 6).

> How our sin degrades and mocks us! It seems attractive to us to satisfy lust or to live without concern for any morality. Yet look at the price-tag! This young man found that sin cost him his self-respect and his happiness.

The son then went into a far country and 'wasted his possessions with prodigal living' (v. 13). Just exactly where all his money went we are not told, but the later reference to 'harlots' (v. 30) is the way our Lord expected the story to be taken. Our sins can leave us in rags (Prov. 23:21) and the prodigal son had the same experience. A famine came, and so desperate was the young man's situation that he became a farmhand, feeding pigs. These animals were considered unclean under Jewish law (Lev. 11:7), and therefore such work was all the more humiliating.

Eventually the young man became hungry for pigswill! How our sin degrades and mocks us! It seems attractive to us to satisfy lust or to live without concern for any morality. Yet look at the price-tag! This young man found that sin cost him his self-respect and his happiness.

It was then he 'came to himself' and remembered that he had a home. He had a caring father and used to eat nourishing food, so he decided to go back, not as a son, but as a servant. He would ask nothing but low-status employment in his father's business. Shortly afterward, the father saw a figure in the distance. Imagine, the young man so much thinner now—perhaps barely recognizable. He ran to his lost boy. He did not stand still reprovingly in the dignity which was rightfully his, but ran to his son, embraced him and threw a party for him.

The elder brother, as would be typical in such circumstances, was less impressed, seeing no reason for celebration. Yet the father had to teach him something about the joy of a restoration. The past, the foolishness, the squandering of a small fortune was all forgotten. Not one reference is made to it by the father.

In this parable Jesus conveyed something of the great and deep love of God. Returning backsliders are welcomed by their Heavenly Father. Come to him if as yet you have never trusted in him. What a welcome awaits the broken-hearted sinner! What joy! What acceptance! What comfort!

FOR FURTHER STUDY

1. The term 'backsliding' is found only in the Old Testament. Where does it occur?
2. The Bible gives many pictures of the cost of sin, even for believers: Samson without eyes; the prodigal son starving in a pig farm; Peter weeping bitterly. Why do we still love sin?
3. Luke 15:30. The prodigal son may have been brought to poverty through encounters with prostitutes. Why are sexual sins so destructive? (See Prov. 6:23-26 and 1 Peter 2:11.)

TO THINK ABOUT AND DISCUSS

1. In the light of this parable, can large sums of money destroy the lives of the young?
2. In what way is every repentant sinner like the prodigal son?
3. What characteristics of the bitter older brother do we possess? In what circumstances might you see them?

16 Luke Chapter 16

This is perhaps one of the strangest parables ever spoken by the Lord Jesus. A steward is fired for wasting his master's goods. So, he immediately tells everyone who owes his master oil or wheat to reduce their bill and write off some of the amount.

Business sense (16:1-13)

It seems very odd that a devious steward would be commended by his employer for altering what was owed to his master (vv. 8, 9). Some see this parable simply as the crooked steward continuing to swindle his master for his own benefit.

Yet it seems to me, considering not only the parable, but the words of our Lord directly afterwards, that the steward 'made friends' with money (see vv. 9-12) by paying the difference himself. It seems that by implication the steward invested fifty measures of oil and twenty measures of wheat into his own future. He gave so that he would later receive kindness from those indebted to his master.

This would help to explain why Jesus spoke of the

importance of 'faithfulness in unrighteous mammon'[11] and being 'faithful in what is another man's' (vv. 11, 12). When we give sacrificially we shall reap future benefit as we receive treasure in heaven. In this way, even 'unrighteous mammon' becomes our friend (v. 9). Our Lord ends by saying 'you cannot serve God and mammon' (v. 13). If you desire to serve God, you must make friends of mammon by investing it in the kingdom, not just using it for your pleasure.

FOR FURTHER STUDY

1. In Luke 16:13 and Matthew 6:24, Jesus reveals we can end up serving wealth as a slave. We might say we can love God and mammon. Yet Christ says if we are 'loyal' to God we will 'hate' mammon. What are the practical implications of these verses for us?
2. Look up 1 Timothy 6:10. How many evils can you attribute to the love of money?
3. Consider Delilah (Judg. 16:4, 5) and Judas (Luke 22:4-6). What sins are people willing to commit for the right price?

TO THINK ABOUT AND DISCUSS

1. 'The sons of this world are more shrewd in their generation than the sons of light '(v. 8). In what instances can you see this today?
2. If the best investment is in the kingdom of heaven, why are we so slow to obey?
3. 'The Bible isn't balanced when it talks about "mammon". We need money to live!' How would you answer this?

Understanding the law (16:14-18)

It is interesting to see what our Lord's teaching drew out of people. His teaching often met with stiff opposition. The Pharisees, who 'were lovers of money', derided Jesus. Material things are highly esteemed among men, yet such things are an abomination to God (v. 15).

The Lord continued, however, by showing that not all will baulk at his sayings. The standard is high, but there are those who will not let that prevent them from entering the kingdom. Many will press into it (v. 16). He stated that the Law of God has abiding force (v. 17). By this he meant the moral law, such as the ten commandments which were further summarized in having love for God and one's neighbour. Throughout his ministry, Jesus quoted from the law as having abiding value. Indeed, we know from Paul that the law is our 'schoolmaster' or 'tutor' to bring us to Christ (Gal. 3:24). The Law, in all its severity, points to the need for atonement and forgiveness, teaching us that we all need to be clothed in the righteousness of another (Rom. 10:4). Thus the law has eternal value.

Finally, the Lord spoke concerning marriage. The Pharisees had allowed for easy divorce through Moses' permission. Yet here, Christ taught that the marriage vows were binding for life.

Roles reversed: the rich man and Lazarus (16:19-31)

This parable followed on from our Lord's teaching concerning the law (cf Luke 16:17, 31). This parable is unique, since it is the only story Jesus told in which a name is given: Lazarus. (This is not the same man whom our Lord raised to life in John 11.)

The rich man 'fared sumptuously every day'—he had wonderful food. Yet a poor beggar, Lazarus, desired to be fed with crumbs from his table. He also had a dreadful disease of the skin. Eventually the beggar died, and was carried by angels to 'Abraham's bosom'. Aside perhaps from Elijah's remarkable ascension, this is the only place in Scripture that speaks of a convoy of angels carrying a man to heaven.

Throughout his ministry, Jesus quoted from the law as having abiding value. Indeed, we know from Paul that the law is our 'schoolmaster' or 'tutor' to bring us to Christ (Gal. 3:24).

Of the rich man, it simply says, 'The rich man also died and was buried'. But then, Jesus shows us their respective places after death—a terrifying picture, for we see the rich man in hell, crying out to Abraham even for a drop of water. For some reason he seemed to think Lazarus might act the part of a servant and bring him aid, or later visit his relatives. However, all that was past. The beggar was blessed and the rich man tormented.

A 'great gulf' (v. 26) separated them. The parable does not mean that the rich will always be excluded from heaven or that the poor will always be taken there. Instead, in this particular case, we see a remarkable reversal of roles. What a hopeless picture for the rich man! What an inversion of everything he had known on earth! 'Now he is comforted and you are tormented' (v. 25).

Finally the rich man asked that his five brothers be warned about future torment. The Lord Jesus wanted us to see that heaven and hell are places inhabited by conscious souls at this present moment. These states are concurrent with life on earth. (See the questions based on Luke 23:43.)

A major aspect of the parable is to show the sufficiency of the word of God. A man might rise from the dead and warn others about hell; yet, unless his hearers believe in the truth of the Scriptures, they will not be persuaded 'though one rise from the dead' (v. 31). This was borne out by the way the religious leaders reacted to the resurrection of the other Lazarus, brother to Mary and Martha, when they simply plotted to kill him (John 12:9-11)!

FOR FURTHER STUDY

1. In the light of Luke 16:15 and 1 Corinthians 1:26-29, what does God think of worldly ambition and fame?
2. Consider Luke16:18. Look up the following texts as they relate to divorce and remarriage: Matthew 19:1-12; Mark 10:1-12; Romans 7:2, 3; 1 Corinthians 7:39, 40.
3. Look at Luke 16:22ff. Heaven and hell are present realities, and do not just exist in the future. Otherwise Enoch and Elijah went nowhere when they ascended to heaven. Additionally, such texts as Revelation 6:9-11 show that life on earth is concurrent with life in heaven.
4. Why is it hard for the rich to enter heaven? (See Luke 16:22, 23 and 18:25.)

TO THINK ABOUT AND DISCUSS

1. Refer to Luke 16:15. Write a list of things that are highly esteemed in the world. How many of them are 'abomination in the sight of God'? How far have we succumbed to secular thinking?
2. In Luke 16:20, 21, the rich man at least allowed the unsightly beggar Lazarus to remain at his gate and receive food from his table. How would you react if such a man lay at your front door, or by your church gates, every day? Are we even more hard-hearted than the rich man?
3. Read Luke 16:31 again. Do we really believe in the sufficiency of Scripture to save and warn today?

17 Luke Chapter 17

Each individual stands or falls alone. We are used to considering our own individual accountability before God, yet here the Lord Jesus went further, saying that those who tempt others to sin, or cause them to stumble, are to be held particularly accountable.

Sin and its consequences (17:1-4)

He issued a warning which he applied to those who sin against 'little ones' (see Matt. 18:6, 7). How terrible on the Day of Judgement for those who have caused others, especially children, to stumble in their spiritual lives. We learn here also that future judgement is so severe, that even the horror of drowning in the sea is to be preferred to it.

The Lord proceeded to speak of the importance of forgiveness. This may suggest that an unforgiving spirit can also become a stumbling block to others. Believers are to forgive even up to seven times in a day. Here the Lord stressed that we are to forgive those who are sorry for what they have done. In Mark 11:25, 26 he implies that we are to forgive even those who might not have apologized for their wrongdoing.

Just in case we think that the 'seven times' is a limit upon our forgiveness, when Peter quoted these words as a limitation, Jesus replied, 'I do not say to you up to seven times, but up to seventy times seven' (Matt. 18:21, 22). What he clearly meant was an indefinite number, just as God has had mercy on us, and forgiven more sins than we could calculate. We are to be merciful, just as our Father also is merciful (Luke 6:36).

Faith and duty (17:5-10)

Hearing the Saviour speak of forgiveness, the apostles asked, 'Increase our faith'. This request reveals that they thought of him as more than just a Rabbi or even Messiah. Only God is the giver of faith; only he could increase it. The Lord's answer suggests that their need was not so much *great faith* as to ask themselves if they had *any* real faith at all! To him, their faith was smaller than a mustard seed. However, even then it could accomplish great things.

Not only did they need faith, but faith had be exercised. When did they last use their faith to uproot a tree? Great acts of faith are not to be commended as very special; all they required was faith the size of a mustard seed. Nor is it that our acts of righteousness are to be especially noted. Servants are not especially thanked that they have done their duty in the field; rather, they are told to go on serving when they get home, and feed their employer. Are such servants thanked? Jesus says, 'I think not' (v. 9). Indeed their masters very rarely praise them for their duty. The Saviour does not want us to think that we are special simply by doing what is required.

This is to govern our thinking: 'We are unprofitable servants. We have done what was our duty to do' (v. 10).

FOR FURTHER STUDY

1. Sins against children are regarded as very serious by our Lord (see Matt. 18:6-9). How far should these words affect the sentencing of child-abusers today?
2. When Christ was crucified, he prayed for the forgiveness of those who had not repented (Luke 23:34). Is this expected of us? See also Mark 11:25, 26 and Acts 7:60.
3. 'Truly righteous people should never boast of their good deeds.' How far must this be so in the light of Luke 17:10 and Isaiah 64:6?

TO THINK ABOUT AND DISCUSS

1. Read Luke 17:1, 2. Give some examples of where believers might cause others to stumble in their spiritual lives.
2. Look at Luke 17:1. How serious a sin is it if your lifestyle puts someone off from following Christ?
3. If we forgive someone countless times in a day, it implies the person's 'repentance' is shallow or non-existent. How far should our forgiveness depend on the repentance of the other person?
4. 'In the light of Luke 17:6, our faith must be microscopic!' Do you agree?
5. Consider Luke 17:10. How far does the modern believer require praise and recognition in order to be willing to serve God?
6. At funerals, do you think we magnify the deeds of the deceased more than we should? Answer this in the light of Luke 17:10.

Ten to one (17:11-19)

The Lord saw ten lepers as he travelled toward Jerusalem. He was about to endure the most immense suffering. It was the greatest and most terrible ordeal ever to face a man: the cross and the judgement of God for sin. Yet our Saviour did not allow his inner suffering to blind him to the needs of others. Ten lepers, following the regulations of Leviticus 13:46, lived apart from the community and 'stood afar off' (v. 12). They cried out, 'Jesus, Master, have mercy upon us!'

Christ sent them to the priest for cleansing, that the rituals of Leviticus 14 might be followed. (Leviticus 14 taught about the need for blood to be shed to set us free, and other aspects of our Lord's atonement in symbolic form. See notes on Luke 5:14.)

As they went to the priest, they were set free from leprosy—surely something that would have filled them with gratitude. Yet, nine never returned thanks to the Lord. It seems so ugly that they would forget his kindness so soon, and yet we can all be guilty of such an attitude.

Watch! (17:20-37)

How much is contained in these eighteen verses! They tell us all we need to know to prepare for the Second Coming of the Lord Jesus Christ.

It will be visible and unmistakeable

The Lord pointed out that many would say the Messiah had appeared in some particular location on this earth (v. 23). Believers, however, were to remember that his coming would be as sheet lightning that flashes out of one part of heaven and shines across the sky. No one would be left in any doubt as to whether the Messiah had returned.

Jesus continued, however, to address the great error of those who anticipated that the Messiah would establish an earthly kingdom and world peace the first time he came. Discernment was required in order to recognize which prophecies related to the first and which to the second coming of the Lord. The Jews expected the coming of the Messiah to usher in a time of world peace, yet they were confusing prophecy concerning his first coming with that concerning his second:

His first coming was not visible to all (Luke 17:20)

His first coming was in order to suffer (Isa. 53; Ps. 22; Ps. 69; Zech. 11:12, 13; 12:10).

The second time he will come to reign visibly over all creation (Isa. 2:1-4; 11:6-9).

He was to 'suffer many things and be rejected of this generation' (v. 25).The Lord Jesus had to come as a suffering Messiah, laying down his life so that multitudes from every nation might belong to his kingdom.

It will be unexpected

Christ used no fewer than eight illustrations to prove this. Why did he use such vivid and varied examples, including Noah, Lot, Lot's wife, women grinding at the mill, two men in the field? Clearly, the Lord wanted us to be ready. We must not, like the world that drowned in the days of Noah, live as we like; for an hour of judgement is coming. We must not, like Lot's wife, look back once we have said that we have forsaken this world.

The Saviour concentrated on that great day itself, rather than events which were to precede it. It would be so sudden and unexpected that around the world people would be going about their ordinary business. One would be taken (to be with the Lord) and the other left behind for the coming judgement.

Along the way, Jesus gave hints as to how we should prepare. He said we should not listen to anyone who claimed the Messiah lived in some part of the earth.

We need to prepare

Along the way, Jesus gave hints as to how we should prepare. He said we should not listen to anyone who claimed the Messiah lived in some part of the earth (v. 23). We should be ready to abandon all that we own at a moment's notice (vv. 31-36).

Lot's wife became a pillar of salt (Gen. 19:26) simply for looking back at Sodom. We must not love this world, for one day it will be destroyed (1 John 2:15). Instead we must be willing to leave it behind us, prepared at any time to lose our lives for the Lord's sake (v. 33).

FOR FURTHER STUDY

1. See Luke 17:15-18. Many times during Jesus' ministry he noted that the faith and kindness of an outsider was greater than among the Jewish people (e.g. Luke 7:6-9; 10:33). This is also implied in Ezekiel 3:5-7.
2. Consider again Luke 17:15-18. How far does God expect those who have been delivered from a trial, or healed, to render thanks to him? (See Ps. 107:21 and the case of King Hezekiah's recovery from illness, 2 Chron. 32:24-26.)
3. Consider Luke 17:26-36 in the light of Luke 21:34, 35. The coming of the Lord Jesus will be sudden and unexpected. Look up 1 Thessalonians 5, particularly verses 1-6. He will return as a 'thief in the night'. Yet notice, however, that Paul believed that God's people should be in readiness. For the believer that great day will not be unexpected (1 Thes. 5:4).

TO THINK ABOUT AND DISCUSS

1. Suggest some ways in which believers might express gratitude to God for healing from sickness.
2. If you knew that the Lord Jesus were to return in thirty days, how different would your life be? What would you do differently? Is it fair to say that this describes how we should spend every period of thirty days?
3. Luke 17:34-36. 'Today we fool ourselves that we are ready for the return of Jesus'. Are we?

18 Luke Chapter 18

Earlier in his ministry, our Lord had taught simple lessons in prayer. However, we always have more to learn. Here are two parables which shed great light upon this vital subject. Both of these parables are found only in Luke.

The persistent widow (18:1-8)

The first parable deals with the subject of persistence in prayer. A widow sought help from an 'unjust judge'. In the days of the New Testament people petitioned judges much as today they would a Member of Parliament or a Senator. There may perhaps be a subtle jibe here at the fact that so many officials have disregard for man and no fear of God!

The judge refused to listen to her at first, but eventually her persistence won the day and he gave in. The Lord used the example of this unjust judge as a strong *contrast* to the true and living God. God is not unwilling to help us. Rather, he measures our concern for a particular matter by our persistence and he will indeed speedily avenge his chosen people. Christ ended on a very solemn note. 'Nevertheless, when the Son of Man comes, will he really find faith on the earth?' (v. 8). This implies that faith is often strengthened by waiting on God and persistence in prayer, even if we do not receive immediate answers. Job had faith to recognize the goodness of God even when, humanly speaking, all seemed lost (Job 23:8-10).

The Pharisee and the tax collector (18:9-14)

This parable deals with the *content* of our prayers. Here are two men who went to the Temple. The Pharisee was ostentatious in his posture during prayer, by implication raising his eyes to heaven (see v. 13). How important it is that we approach God humbly. When we refer to ourselves in prayer, it should be to confess our sins, not boast of our virtues!

Outwardly, the Pharisee was holy. He lived a good, religious, moral way of life. Yet God had no time for his self-centred gratitude.

Outwardly, the Pharisee was holy. He lived a good, religious, moral way of life. Yet God had no time for his self-centred gratitude. The tax collector (or 'publican') on the other hand, just beat his breast, saying 'God, be merciful to me a sinner!' This second man 'humbled himself' and went home 'justified' (v. 14)—that is, God proclaimed him as righteous in his sight. Why? Because of his humility before God. The Pharisee, however, was still in his sins, however good he appeared to men.

FOR FURTHER STUDY

1. To be 'justified' means to be 'proclaimed righteous' (v. 14). It is important that we understand this term, for it is used many times in Scripture. It means more than 'forgiven'—it means that the person is to be regarded as good. If it meant 'forgiven' it could not apply to God, because he has never sinned. Yet the Scripture tells us we can 'justify God' (Luke 7:29) that is, proclaim him righteous.
2. Consider Luke 4:18 and 18:13-14. Also look up Isaiah 66:1, 2. What does God most delight to see?

TO THINK ABOUT AND DISCUSS

1. Read Luke 18:1 again. George Muller spent over sixty years praying for two people to be saved.[12] Do we have this degree of commitment?
2. How can we best develop faith in God?
3. Luke 18:14. Are we humble in our prayers? When does public gratitude to God become pride?

Children first (18:15-17)

Children were brought to the Lord for him to bless them. The disciples tried to protect him from this intrusion upon his time—yet he rebuked them. In fact, Mark 10:14 records that he was 'greatly displeased' that the disciples had sought to keep children away. He welcomed the little children, and made it clear that, far from their characteristics irritating him, only those who received God's kingdom as little children would enter in. There are characteristics of little children which should be imitated: their acceptance of truth, their willingness to forgive, their joy in simple things. Are you like a little child?

Sacrifices for the Kingdom (18:18-30)

Almost is not enough (18:18-23)

Matthew recorded that this ruler was young (Matt. 19:20, 22) and Mark wrote that he came running to Jesus and kneeled before him (Mark 10:17). Here was a very zealous and enthusiastic man. He asked, 'Good teacher, what shall I do to inherit eternal life?'

Our Lord's response to this man seems off-putting. First he rebuked him for calling him 'good'. This is because the Lord Jesus would not accept empty flattery. He stood there as God 'manifest in the flesh' (1 Tim. 3:16) and wanted the rich man to understand who it was he was addressing—not just a 'good teacher' but God himself.

Jesus continued by testing him. He compared his life to the perfect standard of the law of God, running through half of the ten commandments. The rich man was convinced of his own righteousness: 'All these things I have kept from my youth' (v. 21).

The final test was too great for the man. It was an application of the tenth commandment 'Thou shalt not covet' (Exod. 20:17, AV). The medicine was too strong for him: 'You still lack one thing. Sell all that you have and distribute to the poor, and you will have treasure in heaven; and come, follow me.'

We might think that to test the man to breaking point

showed a lack of compassion on the part of Jesus. Yet Mark wrote that the Saviour 'loved him' (Mark 10:21). These were not words to destroy but to bless the man. Three great truths emerge.

A RIGHTEOUS PERSON cares for the poor. Christ did not teach the renouncing of possessions for its own sake, but to give to those in need.

A TRUE CHILD OF GOD will want to lay up treasure not on earth but in heaven. Our hearts are where our treasure lies (Matt. 6:21).

A TRUE FOLLOWER OF GOD will desire to follow Jesus.

The rich man 'became very sorrowful'. His possessions were too precious to renounce. Ultimately riches do not add to our enjoyment but diminish from it.

The wealth trap (18:24-30)

For a moment the Lord also became sorrowful, warning the disciples in no uncertain terms that 'it is easier for a camel to go through the eye of a needle than for a rich man to enter the kingdom of God.' Christ clearly wanted us to see the obstacles that confront the wealthy. What follows does not diminish this statement, but shows that by a miracle he can even open the way for the rich to enter heaven.

Peter, who so often spoke out on behalf of all the disciples, said, 'See, we have left all and followed you'. The Lord replied that all that one forsook for the kingdom would be made up to us many times over in this life, and in the age to come there would be eternal life.

The cross will come (18:31-34)

Who could imagine a clearer, more vivid statement of events yet to come than we find here? The Lord Jesus spoke in the plainest terms. 'All things that are written by the prophets concerning the Son of Man will be accomplished' (v. 31), a vivid description of the pre-execution mocking, spitting and scourging. He said that they would 'kill him. And the third day he [would] rise again'. The Son of God spoke of his death many times, sometimes teaching specifically that it would be by crucifixion (Matt. 20:19); yet still the disciples found his words almost impossible to comprehend. The words were spoken, but the meaning 'was hidden from them' (v. 34). Only after his resurrection did they recall what he had said. God hid the meaning from them. It is his privilege to conceal truth (see Luke 10:21).

> It is wonderful to consider that, despite the crowds, our Lord had time for the needs of individuals.

The man who refused to be quiet (18:35-43)

A blind man begged by the roadside. When he heard that the Master was passing by, he sought to get his attention; 'Jesus, Son of David, have mercy on me!' (Luke 18:38).

All three synoptic Gospels record this account of the blind man receiving his sight, and all three mention that when he was rebuked for shouting he cried out even more. Mark gives his name: Bartimaeus (Mark 10:46). It is wonderful to consider that, despite the crowds, our Lord had time for the needs of individuals. 'Jesus stood still' (v. 40). He asked the blind man, 'What do you want me to do for you?' So often during our Lord's ministry he wanted people to articulate their need. Isn't this the whole meaning of prayer? Prayer is the offering up of our desires to God. He is already more than aware of them, but wants us to specify our requests (see Phil. 4:6).

The Lord said, 'Receive your sight', and Bartimaeus was healed. His faith had reached out to the Lord and now, through the mercy shown to him, his blindness had gone. Afterwards not only Bartimaeus but the whole crowd gave glory to God. How important it is that we recall the goodness of God in restoring health, and praise him for it!

FOR FURTHER STUDY

1. Consider Luke 18:15-17. Look up what was said about children in Luke 7:32 and Luke 9:47, as well as 1 Corinthians 13:11 and Ephesians 4:14. Note that there are characteristics of children to be imitated, and some to be avoided.
2. Look again at Luke 18:31-34. Biblical prophecy is very precise. In 1 Kings 13:2 the name of king 'Josiah' and his actions were prophesied almost three hundred years before his birth. Peter's martyrdom was predicted in John 21:18, 19. Likewise, in Zechariah 11:12, 13 and Psalm 22:1, 16-18, we see detailed predictions of the betrayal and suffering of Christ.
3. Read Luke 18:43. How essential is it for us to give God glory when we have been healed, and to tell others? (See also Isa. 38, 2 Chron. 22:34-26 and Luke 8:38, 39.)

TO THINK ABOUT AND DISCUSS

1. Look up Luke18:15-17. Are we childlike in our response to Christ?

2. Consider Luke 18:22, 23. Was the rich young ruler more entangled in his possessions than modern believers? Would our response to Christ's command have been different?

3. Refer to Luke18:34. Why were the disciples so slow to understand our Lord's clear predictions of his death? Are there prophecies in Scripture today that are 'hidden' from modern followers of the Lord? Would we even recognize which they are?

19 Luke Chapter 19

For many, Zacchaeus is a figure of fun—a short swindler who adds comic relief to an otherwise serious Gospel. Yet if we look more closely, this account gives a startling insight into the real meaning of conversion, and the way that God works in the heart even before a person is saved.

Anti-social climber (19:1-10)

Zacchaeus belonged to the dishonourable band of tax collectors, who often swindled people out of their money, combining threats with deceit. Such was the occupation of this rich man. He was a chief tax collector, and he would have been familiar with local Roman dignitaries. He had perhaps all but forgotten his Hebrew roots in the mad search after money. Yet the Lord was already at work in his heart for he wanted to see Jesus. This travelling teacher intrigued him. Despite his wealth, he chose the undignified option of climbing a tree to see him. It often happens that those whom the Lord intends to save are made curious to know more about him first.

There is animation and haste in this narrative. He did not

walk to the tree but 'ran' (v. 4). He was energetic in his desire to see Jesus. Perhaps he felt that he would be unseen in the tree, and that Christ would only notice the people around him. Yet, like that other man from the region of Jericho, Bartimaeus (Luke 18:35-43), he caused the Lord to stop.

Zacchaeus may have felt uncomfortable when the Lord called him by name. After all, the crowd clearly knew Zacchaeus' occupation (v. 7). Yet he received the Lord joyfully (v. 6), welcoming Jesus of Nazareth to his home.

The Lord Jesus has promised to return one day. Some do not desire for him to rule over them—in fact, the opinion of many may be that they do not wish for him to return at all. Yet he will come back. On that day will you be ready for him?

The subsequent events show that his heart was truly changed that day. He was determined to serve the Lord from that moment. He was not just going to follow an honest course, but make restitution for the wrongs he had done. He gave to the poor, and restored what he had taken. Far from boasting, his words (see v. 8) are an admission of guilt and a sign of his deep humility before God. For many today, trust in Jesus is simply about wiping the slate clean, and being forgiven—yet it is also about restitution. We must restore all we have stolen, and make peace with those we have hurt.

Jesus taught that we are known by our fruit (see notes on Luke 6:43). Zacchaeus showed, not just by words but also deeds, that he trusted in the Messiah, and was a new person. The Lord Jesus rejoiced that salvation had come to his home, and also remarked that this was all the more fitting because 'he also is a son of Abraham' (v. 9)—not only a son by birth, but now also by faith (Gal. 3:7).

The Saviour ended by saying, 'The Son of Man has come to seek and to save that which was lost' (v. 10). This account makes it clear that a man may be a Hebrew by birth, but still be lost. The Lord specialized in calling not the righteous but sinners to repentance (see Luke 5:31, 32 and Luke 15:4-7).

Investing in the Kingdom: the ten pounds, or 'minas' (19:11-27)

The Lord Jesus gave this parable because the people 'thought the kingdom of God would appear immediately' (v. 11). Here he revealed the various ways people would serve him when he was away. Some desired that he would never return, some lived wisely, investing their time and talents for him, and some did nothing.

This parable is about a harsh nobleman, who, like the unjust judge (Luke 18:1-8) was *in contrast* to the Lord. He was austere and fierce (vv. 21, 22). Throughout this parable we see the importance of patiently serving a Master who expects us to be faithful with what he has entrusted to us.

Before he left, the nobleman handed out ten 'minas' or 'pounds' (AV). He gave ten of his servants one mina each—the equivalent of about three months' salary—telling them to 'do business till I come' (v. 13). He expected them to invest their money wisely and profitably. He was so unpopular that a delegation from his home town was sent with the message that they despised his rule. Yet the day came when he was seen on the horizon. He had come back. On his return he found that the first two had invested at good interest, but the third had simply hidden his coin away.

The Lord Jesus has promised to return one day. Some do not desire for him to rule over them—in fact, the opinion of many may be that they do not wish for him to return at all. Yet he will come back. On that day will you be ready for him?

The nobleman was angry with the servant who just put his money in a handkerchief. He reprimanded him sharply and handed his money over to the one who had been most successful in his trading. The people were amazed at this (v. 25). He astonished them further by executing those who refused his rule. In this way Christ taught the stern justice of judgement day. Those with treasure in heaven would receive more, and those with none would lose what earthly treasure they had. Thus Jesus will be angry with all those who have just sat on the abilities and 'talents' which he has given.

Some see in this parable that the Lord is supporting the wise use of investments and the stock market. Yet in fact, the best investment is in the kingdom, and to have treasure which cannot be touched. Coming as it does straight after the account of Zacchaeus, who had given half of his goods to the poor, surely no one would say that Zacchaeus should have invested his money in the bank! He had made a wise choice, as we see in Luke 18:22. Zacchaeus invested in the kingdom in the same way as the good servant who invested his money wisely.

Lastly, the Lord stresses that if we have treasure when he returns we will be blessed with more, and if we have not, even what we have will be taken from us.

The arrival (19:28-40)

Here we see the unfolding of a vital day in our Lord's ministry. It was the first 'Palm Sunday'. Jesus would enter Jerusalem to rapturous, spontaneous praise. Yet within a week, Jerusalem would ring with the cry, 'Crucify him!'

The detail given by all three of the synoptic Gospel writers concerning the way Christ obtained a donkey may seem unnecessary. However, we are again made aware of our Lord's poverty, and of his lordship over his creatures. The donkey had never borne the weight of a human being before (v. 30). In most cases, animals of this kind require a time for 'breaking in'. Yet the donkey did not so much as flinch as Jesus rode her.

The owners of the donkey may well have known Jesus and believed in him. The words 'The Lord has need of it' (vv. 31, 34) were sufficient reason to let the animal go.

The Lord, however, was not riding a donkey because this was his custom. Instead it was to fulfil prophecy:

> 'Rejoice greatly, O daughter of Zion!
> Shout, O daughter of Jerusalem!
> Behold, your King is coming to you;
> He is just and having salvation,
> Lowly and riding on a donkey,
> A colt, the foal of a donkey' (Zech. 9:9).

The Lord then descended the Mount of Olives, entering Jerusalem from the east. As he did so, the multitude of disciples, perhaps numbering thousands, met him. They threw down their garments as they might have done before royalty, crying, 'Blessed is the King who comes in the name of the Lord!' (v. 38; cf Ps. 118:26). It must have seemed as if the whole of Jerusalem erupted in spontaneous joy as the Lord of glory approached the city.

The Pharisees, by contrast, asked Jesus to rebuke his disciples (vv. 39, 40). John records that they were worried and felt 'the whole world [had] gone after him!' (John 12:19). They could not see that the King of kings was arriving, who deserved infinite praise (see notes on Luke 11:34). Indeed, had the disciples been silent, the very stones would have immediately cried out (v. 40)!

FOR FURTHER STUDY

1. Look up Luke19:8 and compare Exodus 22:1, 4 and Proverbs 6:30, 31. Notice that under Old Testament Law, thieves had to restore more than they took—sometimes five times what was stolen, sometimes four, and sometimes even seven times! Consider how far the principle of restitution should affect our legal system today. How might new converts restore property they may have stolen in the past?
2. Consider Luke 19:8. It seems that a characteristic first step in those who were saved in the New Testament church was that they gave a large proportion of their estate to the needy (see Acts 2:44,45 and Acts 4:32-37). Why has this practice faded out of use today?
3. In Luke 19:30, we see our Lord's sovereignty over creatures that would otherwise kick and fight to have the rider removed. Consider his dominion over creatures in Matthew 17:27 (see also 1 Kings 17:2-6 and Jonah 1:17; 4:6).

TO THINK ABOUT AND DISCUSS

1. Zacchaeus wanted to catch a glimpse of the Lord. What form did your curiosity

about Christ take before you trusted in him?

2. If the best use of our talents is the service of Christ, should every believer seriously contemplate full-time Christian work?

3. How much of our time, talents and treasure should be invested in the kingdom of God?

4. Reflect on Luke 19:31, 34. How far are we willing to forego property or time simply because 'the Lord has need' of it?

5. Refer to Luke 19:39. How far might it be said that Satan hates to hear believers praise their Lord? What opposition to praise might we expect today, and how should we deal with it when it comes?

From triumph to sorrow (19:41-44)

Jerusalem was a city of tremendous privileges. It had witnessed the preaching of prophets such as Isaiah and Jeremiah. It was the place where David and Solomon had ruled so successfully. Most of all, it was the place where the Temple was found, in which the ark of the covenant rested. Jerusalem symbolized the presence and blessing of God. It had been magnificently developed during the reign of Herod the Great. Yet all of that was about to change.

Jesus was praised by an adoring multitude, surrounded by this strong and beautiful city. Everything looked positive—yet he knew that within a week he would be crucified there. He knew also that in forty years, Jerusalem would be destroyed. He could see from the corner of his eye the moneychangers outside the Temple, and knew that this magnificent city was undermined by the cancer of unbelief and sin.

Christ, who came as 'a man of sorrows, and acquainted

with grief', did not allow the joy of the praise to lift his spirits for long. He began to weep over the city. As Jeremiah had wept before and after its destruction six hundred years before, so the Lord Jesus stood beside the same city as a weeping prophet. His cry was over their blindness; 'If you had known, even you, especially in this your day…you did not know the time of your visitation'. It seems the Lord lamented most of all the fact that they did not recognize him as Messiah. He would have reigned over them, instructed them and granted them countless blessings. But they would reject him.

> Christ, who came as 'a man of sorrows, and acquainted with grief', did not allow the joy of the praise to lift his spirits for long.

For this reason, enemies would one day build siege works around the city and 'close you in on every side' (v. 43). In AD 70, Jerusalem was besieged by the Romans after a series of skirmishes with the local population. The city, although equipped to withstand a long siege, had internal strife. The community within its walls was divided into factions. Jerusalem eventually fell to the Romans after just a few months. Much of it was burned with fire. The Temple platform was stormed and the Temple itself destroyed.

Here were a people who had refused to hear God's voice. Soon a punishment would be sent to them which would be remembered throughout time.

The crash of coins (19:45-48)

The same day that the Lord was showered with praise, he

headed for the Temple. Here people sold doves and animals for sacrifice and changed Roman, pagan coins into money which could be used as gifts in the holy temple. Christ did not object to these things *per se*, but to their proximity to the holy place. As Nehemiah had dealt harshly with Tobiah, a pagan who had been given room in the Temple, and threw him out with his possessions (Neh. 13:4-8), so the Lord here drove the men out by force. On an earlier occasion, Jesus had made a whip of small cords to drive the men out (John 2:13-17) but it seems they had resumed business as usual.

Perhaps as a result of the events of Palm Sunday, the authorities in Jerusalem became more desperate to destroy Jesus (vv. 47, 48). They were alarmed at his popularity, stunned by his forthright opposition to their practices, and wanted this man to be out of the way.

FOR FURTHER STUDY

1. Look again at Luke 19:41-44. If Jewish people who rejected Jesus as their Messiah were under God's wrath in the first century, has the situation changed today? (See Matt. 27:24, 25, 2 Cor. 3:14-16 and 1 Thes. 2:14-16.) How best can we share the gospel with Jewish friends?
2. The people did not know the time of their visitation. Is there a similar lack of faith when God is at work during periods of revival? Can you think of examples today (see Hab. 1:5)?

TO THINK ABOUT AND DISCUSS

1. Refer to Luke 19:41. How grieved are we over the sins around us? Do we accept the ways of sinners too readily today?

2. Consider Luke 19:42. How much peace the people of Jerusalem would have enjoyed had they trusted in the Prince of Peace! Referring to Isaiah 48:18 and Psalm 38:4, 5, how much peace and joy have we lost through the foolishness of our own sins?

3. Reflect on Luke 19:45, 46. When is it justifiable to use force to rebuke sin?

4. In the light of Luke 19:45, 46, should churches be used to sell goods for profit—even Bibles and Christian materials?

20 Luke Chapter 20

Some people think that the Lord Jesus answered every question put to him. Actually, he wanted to guide the questioner away from idle thoughts to consider what really matters. The Lord does not want to do all our thinking for us.

Jesus is challenged (20:1-8)

In the opening verses of Luke 20, three groups of Jewish leaders confront Jesus with the question, 'Tell us, by what authority are you doing these things? Or who is he who gave you this authority?' He could easily have replied that his Father in heaven had given this authority, and proceeded to question them about their own obedience to the Father. He wanted, instead, to reveal their fear of being undermined or hated. Therefore he asked them about the baptism of John. We know that the ministry of Jesus was connected to that of his forerunner, John. The opening chapters of Luke reveal this plainly by closely relating the events of the two births, and the relationship of Mary to Elizabeth.

Their answer (v. 7), although politically neutral, reveals ignorance and fear. Jesus had refused to give a direct answer to those who sought to trap him. Instead they are trapped by their own hypocrisy.

Keep out! (20:9-19)

God's ways astound us. In this parable of the vineyard, we see his great mercy, and also his justice. What is particularly striking is that, on hearing this solemn parable, 'the chief priests and scribes that very hour sought to lay hands on him' (v. 19).

In this parable (like that of the ten minas in chapter 19), the illustration relates to God the Father who has planted a 'vineyard'. (In Isaiah 5:1-7, the picture of a vineyard refers to Israel.) God looks for good produce; yet instead of sweet grapes, 'wild grapes' grow there. God's people, the 'vinedressers', refuse to give the fruit required, beat the three servants he sends to them, the last being 'wounded' and cast out. This represents the prophets sent by God to warn his people. They treat them shamefully, and in each case no fruit is returned to the owner. At last he sends his 'beloved son', saying, 'Probably they will respect him when they see him' (v. 13). He is not only rejected, but murdered. In some way the vinedressers imagined that this would be a way to receive the inheritance. It may be that those who called for the Lord's crucifixion thought that Israel would gain from his condemnation. In fact, it led to their destruction, and the removal of their vineyard, Israel, for two millennia. It would take more than nineteen centuries before the people of Israel would be a nation once more.

Jesus applied the words of Psalm 118:22 to himself. Like a stone which builders reject, which later stands proudly as 'the chief cornerstone', he then, formidably, warns that those who reject him will be destroyed. Similar language surrounds our Saviour's return as judge in Psalm 2:9:

'You shall break them with a rod of iron;
You shall dash them in pieces like a potter's vessel.'

As already noted, the chief priests and the scribes recognized themselves in this parable. What is particularly disturbing is that, instead of repenting of their lack of fruit and welcoming the son, they sought to fulfil the parable by destroying him!

FOR FURTHER STUDY

1. With reference to Luke 20:2-8, look up other places where Jesus refused to answer a direct question, such as Luke 13:23, 24 and John 18:33, 34.
2. Consider Luke 20:10-13. How much blood was on the hands of Jesus' hearers, according to Luke 11:49-51?
3. Look up Luke 20:17 and Psalm 118:22. How few really understand the greatness and glory of the Lord Jesus! During his ministry, he sometimes appeared to be weak, as a stone which builders might reject (Isa. 53:2). His people did not understand him (John 1:10-12). One day we will see him exalted above all (Acts 4:12; Phil. 2:8-11; 1 Cor. 15:24-26).

TO THINK ABOUT AND DISCUSS

1. Consider Luke 20:5-7. How far are our views shaped by our fear of what others think of us?

Look again at Luke 20:10. God has the right to expect our lives to be fruitful. What kind of fruit does he expect from us today?

2. Why is it that some who hear predictions of their own future sins proceed to do them all the more (Luke 20:19)?

Taxes to Caesar (20:20-26)

> However, more importantly, the Most High God has put his image upon us and we must give him what is rightfully his, and serve him with our entire being.

In Jerusalem, the religious leaders were growing desperate. Here was a rabbi who seemed so popular that he was beyond their power to silence. We are told that 'they watched him' as they had done many times before (see Luke 20:20 and Luke 14:1). Already, they feared popular opinion (vv. 6, 19). John 12:19 makes it clear that they said to one another on Palm Sunday, 'You see that you are accomplishing nothing. Look, the world has gone after him'.

As an act of desperation, spies were sent to trap the Lord. They began by flattering him (v. 21) saying they regarded him as a good rabbi, for he showed no favouritism, but taught 'the way of God in truth'. Having sweetened the trap, they proceeded to try to make him stumble. Their question about taxes reveals some very clever thinking. If he said, 'Pay taxes' and was seen as a friend of the Romans, his popularity among the people might have waned. If he declared taxes should *not* be paid, it would be easy to induce the Romans to arrest him. Could he get out of this one?

For all the brilliance of the question, it is our Lord's answer that is best remembered. He who is the source of all wisdom (Col. 2:2, 3) gave the most remarkable answer. He asked for a denarius, upon which the face of Tiberius would be clearly seen. The Lord said, 'Render therefore to Caesar the things that are Caesar's, and to God the things that are God's.'

The spies were unable to corner him. Instead, they 'marvelled at his answer' (v. 26). Here he taught that Caesar should have what belonged to him. His own image was on these discs of silver, and if he wanted some back, it was to be given to him. However, more importantly, the Most High God has put his image upon us and we must give him what is rightfully his, and serve him with our entire being. Included also is a sense of the importance of giving God what is his due from our money, by giving generously to the work of his kingdom and to the poor.

A question about the resurrection (20:27-40)

The Sadducees were a sect of Jews who denied the resurrection. In Acts 23:8, Luke gives a fuller picture of their beliefs—they said that there is no resurrection, and no angels or spirits. They tried to have a form of Judaism which was almost entirely secular, and rooted to this world.

The Sadducces brought Jesus a brilliantly thought-out question which was designed to make the doctrine of the resurrection seem absurd. Under the law of Moses, if a man died childless, his brother should marry the widow, and raise up children for his deceased brother (see Deut. 25:5-10).

There was a severe stigma attached to any man who refused to perform this task. The Sadducees told the story of seven brothers who each in turn married one woman. 'In the resurrection,' they asked, 'whose wife does she become? For all seven had her as wife' (v. 33).

Jesus' answer is designed not to sound clever but to be the plain truth. He spoke of the resurrection as something for those 'counted worthy' (v. 35). Although there is no marriage, men and women serve God in wholehearted devotion. They are, in this sense, like the angels, and equal to them (v. 36).

The Lord proceeded to enforce the truth of the resurrection, using as a proof text words which people might not have considered in this light before. Moses at the burning bush called the Lord 'the God of Abraham, the God of Isaac, and the God of Jacob' (v. 37). These men, though dead at the time of Moses, still served the living God. He was their God. In this sense none is 'dead' for 'all live to him' (v. 38). For believers, death will be the glorious moment when they enter life such as they have never known it before.

Some of the scribes who overheard the Lord's answer to the Pharisees said, 'Teacher, you have spoken well'. The questioning stopped, and no one dared ask him questions anymore.

More about the Messiah (20:41-47)

The Lord reminded the people that they rightly expected the Messiah to be the son of David. Jesus descended from David as Luke recorded in chapter 3. This is not the whole picture, however, for David had referred to him as 'Lord'. This expression implies far more than just 'ruler'; indeed for the Jewish people, it was the most frequently used expression for God.

Jesus is the 'Root and the Offspring of David' (Rev. 22:16). He existed from eternity past, and therefore is the root of David's family tree. Yet he is also a *descendant* of David, and therefore a 'branch' of his family.

Christ continued by warning against the scribes. He spoke to the disciples, but deliberately made sure it was 'in the hearing of the people'. He warned the same people who had said, 'Teacher, you have spoken well' (v. 39). He was not taken in by their flattery. He warned that the scribes, who were expert copyists of the Hebrew scriptures, loved the praise of men.

From ancient times the service of God has entailed receiving honours and titles from man to man which belong to God alone. In Matthew 23:8, Christ reminded the scribes and the Pharisees that they ought not to delight in the title 'Rabbi'. Why? For 'one is your Teacher, the Christ, and you are all brethren'. Before God, his people are brethren, and should not seek special titles for themselves.

The scribes exploited the deference paid to them, and they even sought financial gain from poor widows. They liked to appear holy by reciting long prayers. 'Shop window' service to God only drew upon them 'greater condemnation' (v. 47).

FOR FURTHER STUDY

1. In Luke 20 we see the Lord answering difficult questions with great wisdom and power. How far can we ask for this blessing for ourselves, in the light of Luke 21:14, 15?

2. Consider Luke 20:25.The New Testament begins with Joseph and Mary going to Bethlehem to be taxed. Paul teaches that believers must pay every form of taxation (Rom. 13:7). How important to our witness is our willingness to pay tax?

3. Look up Luke 20:27-38. The Old Testament clearly reveals that there is life after death (Dan. 12:2, 3). David knew he would 'dwell in the house of the Lord for ever' (Ps. 23) and Job believed in the resurrection of the body when he would see his Redeemer (Job 19:25-27).

4. Consider Luke 20:34-36. Heaven is a place where God's people do not marry, for they are equal to angels and wholly devoted to him. In the light of Matthew 19:11, 12, 1 Corinthians 7:27-33 and Revelation 14:4, 5, how far can it be said that this is ideally how we should live on earth also?

5. Long prayers were recited to impress others (v. 47). The longest prayer in the Bible (1 Kings 8) takes under ten minutes to read out. As a guideline, what is the right length of public prayers?

TO THINK ABOUT AND DISCUSS

1. Consider Luke 20:24. Jesus had to ask for a coin, and did not seem to have his own money to show them. When he suffered on the cross the soldiers could gamble only for one set of clothes. In Acts 3:5, 6, it is evident that Peter and John had no silver or gold.

2. How reliant on material things should the modern Christian be in our affluent society?

3. Look again at Luke 20:25. What should we 'render to Caesar' and to God today? Explain, in practical terms, what this means.

4. Reflect on Luke 20:27-38. The Bible does not encourage idle speculation about heaven. Paul underlines this in 1 Corinthians 15:33-44. Why does God not entrust us with more detail about our heavenly home?

5. How far can honouring spiritual leaders with titles such as 'Reverend' and 'Father' detract from the glory due to God alone?

21 Luke Chapter 21

Here a widow's secret gift to God became the only deed for which she is remembered. The rich were giving a proportion of their wealth, yet this widow gave all she had. She lived at a time and in a place where the state made no provision for widows.

The widow's two mites (21:1-4)

Yet despite the grave risk to her own welfare, the widow 'out of her poverty put in all the livelihood that she had'. God looks not at the amount, but at the sacrifice involved. It has been said, 'He is no fool who gives what he cannot keep to gain what he cannot lose'.[13]

Tribulation (21:5-38)

In these verses are woven together words concerning the destruction of Jerusalem and the second coming of the Lord Jesus. Sometimes God reveals future, present and past events in one narrative. Hosea 11:1, for instance, speaks of the Exodus of the Israelites from Egypt in approximately 1350

BC, and also the journey of Mary, Joseph and the boy Jesus from Egypt in about AD 5 (Matt. 2:14, 15). Similarly, in the Book of Revelation, amid so many other passages about the future, chapter 12 deals with some events which happened shortly after creation.

In Luke 21:5, remarks are made to Christ about the Temple. Herod the Great (who reigned AD 37-4) had spent a fortune expanding and adorning the Temple area, and all its porches and associated buildings. It was a wonder of the ancient world. Yet, within a generation, all of its beauty would be destroyed by the Roman armies.

The Son of God warned of eight signs of approaching judgement in verses 8-17:

False Christs (v. 8)

Wars and commotions (v. 9)

Nations rising against each other (v. 10)

Great earthquakes in various places (v. 11)

Famines and pestilences (v. 11)

Fearful sights (v. 11)

Great signs from heaven (v. 11)

Persecution of believers (vv. 12-17)

'Great earthquakes in various places' (v. 11) perhaps refers to great tremors in places not usually associated with movements of the earth's crust. 'Fearful sights' (v. 11) might mean that terrifying events will be seen all over the world.

We are assured that, despite fierce persecution, the saints will have nothing to fear. Once more we see our Lord's defiance of death (see notes on Luke 20:38). Although he warned, 'They will put some of you to death' (v. 16), yet ultimately, 'not a hair of your head will be lost' (v. 18). In other words, you will be preserved, and your soul will be secure, even though you may physically die. The same thought is expressed by Paul when, nearing his own death, he wrote, 'I am already poured out as a drink offering, and the time of my departure is at hand'; yet adding, 'the Lord will deliver me from every evil work and preserve me for his heavenly kingdom' (2 Tim. 4:6,18). The soul of the believer is completely safe, even though the body will perish.

Jerusalem in ruins (21:20-24)

God had chosen Jerusalem as the place where his name would dwell (see notes on Luke 19:41-44). Many times in her history, armies had threatened her and stood outside her walls. Sometimes, through the Lord's merciful intervention, danger was averted. For instance, three armies approached in the days of Jehoshaphat (2 Chron. 20). As the people inside the city worshipped the Lord, the troops were struck and turned against one another. In the days of King Hezekiah, over 185,000 troops sent by Sennacherib king of Assyria, came against the city. The army was destroyed by the angel of the Lord.

Would the city be spared next time? No. In Luke 21, the Lord taught that it would be surrounded by armies and destroyed. The emperor Vespasian, weary with Jewish defiance of his army of occupation and skirmishes with the local people, sent his son, Titus, to crush resistance in Israel.

The troops arrived in the spring of AD 70. Jesus had said not one stone of the temple would remain upon another (v. 6). The Temple finally fell on the Sabbath day, 10th August, of that year. The soldiers broke apart each stone of the temple to retrieve the melting gold which they could see in the cracks between the stones. By September, the entire city had been taken and for the most part reduced to burning rubble. One-and-a-half million Jews died.

Christ told those in Judea to flee to the mountains on the day that the armies arrived. The people would need to leave urgently and not look back for their belongings. The ancient historians Eusebius and Epiphaneus recorded that the Christians in Jerusalem, who numbered thousands, took the Lord's words seriously and fled to Pella in the region of Decapolis. Although Jerusalem had been very well fortified and prepared for such an onslaught, factions within the city led to the destruction of supplies and the onset of starvation. The Romans finally broke down the walls, and burnt and levelled the city.

Christ warned that his people might become complacent and sinful as they wait for his return. He took nothing for granted, speaking of sins which we hope would never be found among the people of God.

Jesus said pregnant women and those nursing infants would be the most vulnerable (v. 23). Jerusalem would be destroyed and trampled until the 'times of the Gentiles are fulfilled'.

The last days (21:25-28)

Jesus spoke not only of signs which accompanied the destruction of Jerusalem, but also of signs which will precede his second coming, including:

SIGNS ABOVE: In the sun, moon and stars. The moon reflects light from the sun, and therefore these two luminaries will always affect each other (see Rev. 6:12 and Isa. 30:26).

SIGNS BELOW: On the earth there will be 'distress of nations with perplexity.' The events will lead to general anxiety and bewilderment in the world.

SIGNS IN THE SEA: Jesus speaks of 'the sea and the waves roaring'. Many have wondered what exactly is meant here. The Asian Tsunami in December 2004 made the world think again as to what might be intended !

SIGNS WITHIN: The Lord warns of the inner reaction to these cataclysmic events: 'men's hearts failing them from fear'. Believers, however, are to react differently (v. 28). For believers, especially those who are persecuted for their faith, the arrival of the Messiah thrills them and dispels fear. We can feel the joy as John declares at the end of the New Testament, 'Even so, come, Lord Jesus!' (Rev. 22:20).

The fig tree (21:29-33)

The people were very familiar with the changing appearance of fig trees. When the trees began to bud, they knew that summer was near. In the same way, there would be recognition that the second coming of the Messiah was approaching. Jesus added that heaven and earth would pass away, but not his words. This world and all it contains would pass away with fervent heat (2 Peter 3:10-13). All of its art treasures and libraries will be turned into ashes. The words of Jesus, however, will be *eternally* remembered. We need to treasure them and teach his words carefully to all nations (Matt. 28:20a).

Watch (21:34-38)

Christ warned that his people might become complacent and sinful as they wait for his return. He took nothing for granted, speaking of sins which we hope would never be found among the people of God. Familiar as he was with the sinfulness of human beings, including his people, he warned of the possibility of believers being 'weighed down with carousing, drunkenness, and cares of this life.' Worry about earthly things is a sin placed alongside drunkenness. The word translated 'cares' means literally to be pulled in different directions. How easy to allow almost every day to be filled with anxieties!

Jesus warned that for some, the second coming will be like a trap (v. 35). For the prepared believer it should not be unexpected, or as a thief in the night (1 Thes. 5:1-4). Prepared believers would not only expect Christ's return, but feel no shame as they stood before him (v. 36). In case we should ask how best to prepare for the moment we leave this world, the chapter ends by revealing our Lord's pattern of life as the day of his death approached. By day he sought to teach others, and by night he communed with his Father in the Mount of Olives (vv. 37, 8). What a glorious example he is to his followers!

FOR FURTHER STUDY

1. Refer to Luke 21:16-18. How can we apply the following promises to ourselves and in what situations: Psalm 91:9, 10; Isaiah 43:1, 2; Luke 6:38?
2. Read Luke 21:25-28 again. Some unbelievers are blind to these events (2 Peter 3:4). Is there such blindness today when we talk of 'natural disasters'?
3. Consider Luke 21:34, 35. Lot and his family had to be almost dragged from Sodom (Gen. 19:15, 16). Are we ready at a moment's notice to leave this world?
4. Reflect on Luke 21:35. Sodom felt safe before its destruction (Gen. 19:14). When judgement hung over Nineveh, the people felt safe before Jonah's arrival. The same feeling of false security will exist immediately before our Lord's return (1 Thes. 5:2, 3). How can we break through this complacency?
5. In Luke 21:34-38, the Lord gave his people warnings against drunkenness prior to his return. Is such sinful behaviour a strong temptation even among believers?

TO THINK ABOUT AND DISCUSS

1. Consider Luke 21:1-4. How far should we be willing to risk everything in our giving? (See Luke 12:33, 14:33.)
2. Look up Luke 21:34, 35. In the light of these words, and 1 Peter 5:6, 7, what is the remedy for cares and worries?
3. Think about Luke 21:37. How important is prayer? Should believers occasionally forego sleep in order to pray?
4. When Jerusalem was besieged, believers found safety in escaping. When should Christians leave a city that is under threat of destruction from natural disasters or warfare? Does it ever mean we are deserting the people we try to serve?

22 Luke Chapter 22

It was no coincidence that the Messiah would die at Passover. At the first Passover in Exodus 12, the blood of a lamb sprinkled upon the doorposts and lintel of a house meant that the family inside were safe, and the destroying angel would 'pass over' them. Now it was the Lord Jesus who would shed his blood to shield his people from judgement.

Preparation for Passover 22:1-13

Alongside the preparation for the holy festival of Passover were some very *unholy* activities. The chief priests and scribes were plotting to kill Jesus. How hypocritical! It is so strange that such men could not see that however ceremonially clean they might be, their activities were full of corruption and evil. John 18:28 records that the religious leaders refused to enter Pilate's judgement hall, where they had sent the Saviour, in case they became defiled and were unable to eat the Passover. In Matthew 27:6-8, the thirty pieces of silver which Judas threw back at the leaders were used to buy a field. They could not be used for the temple for they represented the price of blood. Thus men thought they were holy in the sight of God, when in reality they were his enemies!

There is a link between verse 2 and verse 6. The chief priests wanted to kill Jesus, but feared the crowds. If Judas was to betray him to them, it must be 'in the absence of the multitude' (v. 6).

At that time, Satan entered Judas Iscariot. John 12:6 shows how he dipped into the money set aside for the Lord and his disciples. It was perhaps this petty stealing which gradually formed a wedge between Judas and the rest. It then became easy for Satan to take control of him. At a specific moment, the devil entered Judas—when the Lord handed him bread dipped in the dish at the last supper. He told him, 'What you do, do quickly' (John 13:26, 27).

The Passover meal is full of significance, pointing clearly to the death of the Lord Jesus, as the spotless Lamb of God, and his blood which protects us from judgement.

Peter and John were told to look for a man carrying a pitcher of water. It was customary for women to carry water in this way, but not for men. It would not be difficult, therefore, to spot such a man. They had to follow him and ask for the 'guest room', explaining that the 'Teacher' had sent them. Rather like the way the disciples found the donkey, here they were led to the large room in which the Passover meal was to be eaten. Everything was found, just as Jesus had said, and the Passover meal was prepared.

The Passover meal (22:14-23)

The Lord, with bread and a cup of wine, taught the disciples very profound spiritual truths about communion with him and with one another.

The Passover meal is full of significance, pointing clearly to the death of the Lord Jesus, as the spotless Lamb of God, and his blood which protects us from judgement. On the table were also bitter herbs (such as horseradish), which, for Jewish families up to the present day, represent the bitterness of bondage in Egypt (Exod. 12:8). The Lord, however, wanted to use the meal to teach other lessons. He took the cup first (v. 17), and reminded them that the next occasion when he would drink wine would be at the fulfilment of all joy in the 'kingdom of God'.

He then took bread, gave thanks and broke it. He told them, 'This is my body *which is given for you...*' The bread was unleavened, that is, crisp bread made without yeast. This symbolized the haste with which the children of Israel left Egypt (see Exod. 12:11, 15). Also, yeast is often used in the Bible to represent sin (Luke 12:1; 1 Cor. 5:6-8). In this way, the unleavened bread symbolized the sinless body of Jesus.

Lastly he took the cup: 'This cup is the new covenant in my blood *which is shed for you...*' In each case the personal nature of the atonement is emphasized. It is 'for you'. In this sense, the meal was a way of showing that his death was for those who eat the bread and drink the wine. Jesus taught them to 'do this in remembrance of me'. The meal was to be continued, no longer for the sake of the Passover only, but 'in remembrance of me'. From that distant day to this, the church has sought to observe this supper.

As we have so often seen, the Lord was never permitted to enjoy unbroken peace or fellowship even for an hour. Immediately we are told of his awareness that the betrayer was there (v. 21). It was determined that the Messiah would be betrayed, but woe to the betrayer! They 'questioned among themselves' who it would be (v. 23). The disciples did not instantly point to Judas. His crimes had been secret, and they had seen him along with the rest sent into villages and towns to preach (Luke 9:1-6). How terrible that the Lord's friend should so callously betray him.

FOR FURTHER STUDY

1. Refer to Luke 22:1-6. Judas' betrayal of Jesus was prophesied in the Old Testament—see Psalm 41:9; 109:8 and Acts 1:16-20. How far was Judas free to do as he wished? Are we more free, since our individual conduct has not been foretold in Scripture?
2. The Passover lamb had to be 'without blemish' (Exod. 12:5). In 1 Corinthians 5:7, Paul describes Christ's death in this way: 'Christ our Passover was sacrificed for us'. How far can we say that Christ's character, as the Passover lamb, was 'without blemish'? (See John 8:29, 46; Luke 23:4, 13, 14, 39-41.)
3. How far could it be said that the chief priests were like the people described in Isaiah 29:13?
4. Consider Luke 22:14-20. No one, not even Peter, asked whether the bread and wine became the actual body and blood of the Lord. They knew what he meant; the bread and wine represented his body and blood. (See 2 Sam. 23:14-17.)
5. The apostle Paul tells us that it is crucial to examine ourselves before we eat the bread or drink the wine (1 Cor. 11:27-31). Why is it so rare to find churches where

people are encouraged to undergo self examination before they take the bread and wine?

6. Luke 22:22. If God foretells sin, is the fault still with the sinner? See Acts 2:23. God ordained that Jesus should die, but the hands that took him were evil. What other examples can be found in the Scriptures of God's sovereignty and yet man's accountability?

TO THINK ABOUT AND DISCUSS

1. Jesus took the cup and bread and each time 'gave thanks' (v. 17, 19). Are we sufficiently thankful for the food we eat? Does Acts 27:35 teach us that believers should unashamedly and publicly give thanks for food even when we eat in public such as at a canteen or restaurant?

2. How frequently should the Lord's Supper or communion be observed? Some interpret Acts 20:7 to mean that the common practice was to observe it every Sunday. If it is a 'supper' and not a breakfast, should it only be observed in the evening?

Who is the greatest? (22:24-30)

During the meal the disciples began to argue who should be considered the greatest. The Lord again had to emphasize that his kingdom is not of this world (John 18:36). The planet is full of those who want authority over others. The 'kings of the Gentiles' exercise brutal, selfish authority, yet are given the more flattering title, 'benefactors', as though they existed to help the needy. Jesus taught that the greatest Christian is the servant of all. To encourage the disciples, the Lord added that they had a special place among the people of God: they would sit on twelve thrones judging the twelve tribes of Israel.

Peter's denial predicted (22:31-34)

From Peter's point of view, there was no problem. He was willing to go with Jesus both to prison and even to death. He did not sense the devil preparing to turn his life upside down and sift him as wheat. Much later, when he wrote to believers, Peter seemed to have learnt the lesson, saying Satan is like a roaring lion 'seeking whom he may devour' (1 Peter 5:8).

Only the Lord knows what is around the corner for each of us. He has taught us to pray, 'Lead us not into temptation.' We may not sense that there is any spiritual deficiency in ourselves or threat from the devil, yet, thankfully, as with Peter, Christ prays for us (John 17:15; Heb. 7:25).

Towards Gethsemane (22:35-38)

Christ reminded them of the time when he had sent them two-by-two into towns and villages (see Luke 9). He had sent them with no money of their own. Can God be trusted to supply our needs? Here we hear the verdict. 'Did you lack anything?' They answered, 'Nothing'.

Before leaving for Gethsemane, Jesus made sure there were swords (vv. 35-38). This may be puzzling, and yet it seems the reasons are as follows: For twelve men to defend themselves against a whole band of soldiers with just two swords would be ridiculous. The presence of such weapons would normally do more harm than good, and only increase the likelihood of violence. The Lord had very different reasons for ensuring there were swords. He sought an opportunity to teach a non-violent response to evil, and also to heal an injured enemy. It was therefore intended to demonstrate his compassion.

Gethsemane (22:39-53)

'Gethsemane' means 'olive press'. It speaks perhaps more vividly than any other place of the weight of suffering the Lord was to endure. He was crushed in a press of grief and sadness as he anticipated not only the pain of crucifixion the next day, but also the greater suffering of separation from his Father.

> The Lord was submissive to the Father's will—yet in his humanity, he longed that the 'cup' of suffering be removed from him.

Peter, James and John were selected to draw closest to the place where Jesus prayed. He told them to pray to be kept from 'temptation', meaning here 'hard testing'. He went further away, 'about a stone's throw' (v. 41).

He then spoke to his Father in a way which reveals most fully the suffering of his soul. Messianic prophecy reveals something of how Jesus would feel on the cross (see Ps. 22:14-18 and Ps. 69:1-3, 20, 21). It would be beyond any suffering experienced by anyone before or since.

The agony of our Saviour in the tranquil Garden of Gethsemane teaches us something very important about him. He knew that what was prophesied *would come to pass.* He felt agony in anticipation of what had been foretold long before. Do we believe biblical prophecy with such absolute assurance of what will happen in the future? Never judge what God has said about tomorrow by the atmosphere of today.

The Son of God prayed, ‘Father, if it is your will, take this cup away from me. Nevertheless not my will, but yours, be done’ (v. 42). The Lord was submissive to the Father’s will—yet in his humanity, he longed that the ‘cup’ of suffering be removed from him.

An angel came to strengthen him. His own disciples were sleeping and unable to pray for themselves or comfort him. So great was his agony that his sweat fell as drops of blood from his face. Here we enter into a holy place of which, it has been said, we can only approach as far as a stone’s cast.

As Jesus was still speaking to the disciples, a ‘multitude’ came to arrest him. He did not wear clothes which were so distinctive as to separate him from the disciples. Therefore Judas walked up to him and betrayed him with a kiss.

The Gospel of John records that it was Peter who drew a sword and cut off the ear of the High Priest’s servant. The man’s name was Malchus (John 18:10). The Lord immediately healed him, thus demonstrating his love for enemies even in the heat of an arrest. It was also an opportunity which Jesus used to show that ‘all who take the sword will perish by the sword’ (Matt. 26:52). He then questioned them for coming against him ‘as against a robber, with swords and clubs’. They had not seized him by day, for they feared the people (Luke 20:19). They chose the hour of darkness in keeping with their evil motives (v. 53).

When the shepherd was taken, the sheep scattered (Zech. 13:7). Yet, ironically, if he had never been taken the sheep would have been lost for ever.

FOR FURTHER STUDY

1. Look at Luke 22:29, 30 and compare Matthew 19:28. The disciples would sit upon twelve thrones. It seems clear that Matthias, the disciple who replaced Judas, would sit on his throne (see Acts 1:26).
2.Consider Luke 22:39-46 and Psalm 69:19-21. How lonely was the path of Jesus' suffering?
3. 'An angel appeared to him from heaven, strengthening him' (v. 43). Throughout our Lord's ministry, angels appeared: before his birth (Luke 1:26, 27); to the shepherds (Luke 2:8-14); here in Gethsemane; at his resurrection (Luke 24:1-6) etc. Jesus could have called for legions of angels to defend him if he so desired (Matt. 26:53). Consider the role of angels in the light of these Scriptures.
4. The disciples were in no fit state to help Jesus. Paul found that his friends left him in his hour of need (2 Tim. 4:16, 17). Should we rely on other people to support us in a crisis?

TO THINK ABOUT AND DISCUSS

1. Consider Luke 22:31-34. In the light of 1 Peter 5:8, how conscious are we of the activity of Satan? If a 'roaring lion' approached the doors of your church meeting, how 'sober' and 'vigilant' would you be to avoid him?
2. Peter's assessment of his spiritual strength was incorrect (vv. 33, 34). Is ours?
3. Jesus delighted in the Father's will, however difficult (Ps. 40:7, 8). He wanted us to do the same (Luke 11:2). How far do you delight in the will of God? Are you willing to commit the outcome of every prayer to him?
4. Consider Luke 22:43. How do angels help us today? (See Heb. 1:13, 14.)
5. Jesus healed his enemy (v. 51), and rebuked the one who took the sword (Matt. 26:52). How far should believers preach—and practise—non-violence today?

Jesus…who? (22:54-62)

Peter sinned in a way he had never thought possible (vv. 31-34), the test having come from an unexpected quarter. It must have been cold enough to warrant a fire, and Peter wanted to hide himself among those who warmed themselves. Peter must have felt vulnerable after becoming violent and wounding Malchus. Nervous and shaken, he was unprepared to speak out for Jesus when interrogated by servants beside a fire.

The first denial paved the way for the others, just as surely as one sin follows another. God expects us to be honest and unashamed about Christ. The people knew Peter was a disciple (v. 59), for his accent was Galilean. Mark pointed this out, giving us the fullest account of the denials (Mark 14:66-72). Jesus and the twelve were from Galilee and spoke in that way. Peter felt cornered and even, as Mark records, 'began to curse and swear' that he did not know Jesus. When he heard the rooster crow, he remembered the Lord's words, and wept bitterly. Peter was not as strong as he had imagined himself to be.

The first denial paved the way for the others, just as surely as one sin follows another. God expects us to be honest and unashamed about Christ.

Jesus mocked and beaten (22:63-65)

The 'power of darkness' (v. 53) was now overshadowing the Saviour. Whatever protection he had previously experienced in his ministry was now removed. This was just one of several occasions when he was assaulted in this way before the crucifixion.[14] Abuse of a prisoner was illegal under the law of Moses, but such was the fury of Christ's enemies it seems they wanted to inflict pain and humiliation at every opportunity even before sentence was pronounced. This was prophesied in Isaiah 50:6 and 52:14.

Jesus before the Sanhedrin (22:66-71)

Luke writes that daylight was beginning to break. Other Gospel writers indicate it was still technically night time, a period when trials were illegal. Jesus was interrogated as to whether or not he is the Messiah, the Christ. He refused to answer because of their hardness of heart. He would not cast pearls before swine (cf. Matt. 7:6).

Finally he quoted Scripture. In verses 69 and 70, he spoke more plainly, referring to his second coming. The 'son of man' is a reference to the Messiah, from such passages as Daniel 7:13, 14. He also answered clearly that he is the Son of God. The expression 'you say that I am' means literally, 'you have said it out of your own mouth'.

FOR FURTHER STUDY

1. See Luke 22:63-65. We might ask how it was that God the Father allowed such assault to take place. It must be remembered that God has the power not only to restrain sin, but also to step back and allow sin to occur. What can we learn from the following passages: Genesis 20:6, 31:7; Joshua 11:19, 20 and Psalm 76:10?
2 Refer to Luke 22:63-65. Consider these occasions when the Lord was able to walk through hostile crowds unharmed: Luke 4:28-30; John 8:58, 59. Now, his hour had come.

TO THINK ABOUT AND DISCUSS

1. Consider Luke 22:55-62 and compare Luke 9:26. When are we most in danger of denying our Redeemer today?
2. Refer to Luke 22:63-65. How can we best answer the question, 'Why doesn't a God of love always restrain and prevent sin?'
3. Why is it that some spiritual people, when they sin, are not aware of the wrong they have done for a period of time? (For David it took over a year—2 Sam. 11:26, 27 and 12:15.)
4. Reflect on Luke 22:67, 68. When is it right to answer our enemies plainly? When is it wiser to refuse to speak?

23 Luke Chapter 23

Jesus of Nazareth was a high-profile Rabbi, and it seems the Sanhedrin did not believe it prudent to take matters into their own hands and kill him. In the case of Stephen, some months later, the Sanhedrin took it upon themselves to stone him without referring the matter to Pilate at all (see Acts 7).

Christ before Pilate and Herod (23:1-25)

Pilate was the local Procurator and therefore the final arbiter in life or death cases. Christ was therefore brought to him for final sentencing. From Pilate's point of view, the tirade of charges against Jesus (v. 2) seems so overwhelming that he realizes they are borne of blind rage and malice. 'Perverting the nation', 'forbidding to pay taxes to Caesar', calling himself a 'king'—these were the charges. Pilate must have wondered, 'Is this man really guilty of such crimes? Is he insane? Are his accusers wildly mistaken?'

His initial interview with Jesus revealed that he indeed considered himself to be the 'king of the Jews'. Pilate concluded, however, that no crime had been committed, saying, 'I find no fault in this man' (v. 4). His accusers seemed almost demon-possessed in their desperation to have him killed. When they mentioned Galilee, Pilate shrewdly passed the case over to Herod, who had jurisdiction for that region.

In the few verses which follow, we learn a great deal about the ways of Christ. Herod, far from approaching the matter professionally and asking Jesus about the charges made against him, wanted to see a miracle. But Jesus would not indulge his curiosity. He was not a magician or performer and his tremendous strength and integrity shone forth even as he stood silent before his accusers.

The brutality and contempt with which Christ was treated (v. 11) reveals the true nature of Herod. Far from seeking the truth, he wanted only to satisfy his own idle and malicious desires. The reference to the friendship between Pilate and Herod (v. 12) underlines the fact that both men were evil—they merely expressed their wickedness in different ways; Pilate questioned the motives of the Sanhedrin, yet would not risk his own reputation to defend the Lord, whom he knew to be innocent (vv. 14,15). Herod, however, wanted to be entertained with miracles.

Pilate called the chief priests, rulers and the people and told them in no uncertain terms that Jesus was innocent of the charges brought against him (vv. 13-15). He offered a compromise—Roman chastisement with a flagellum, followed by release. Not enough for the religious leaders, they wanted to see the Lord crucified.

Pilate was willing to release a prisoner at the Passover. Barabbas had been arrested for rebellion and murder, yet he would be set free if this was what they requested. They asked for Barabbas to be released and Jesus to be crucified. After three remonstrations with the crowd, Pilate let Barabbas go free, and the narrative concludes, ominously, that 'he delivered Jesus to their will'.

FOR FURTHER STUDY

1. See Luke 22:64. Christ suffered insult and pain. Note, from Isaiah 50:6 and John 10:17, 18, the voluntary nature of his sufferings.
2. Matthew 27:17, 18 records that Pilate knew that Jesus had been handed over because of 'envy'. How should we understand this?
3. The Lord's silence during much of his trial fulfils Isaiah 53:7. What effect, positive and negative, do you think his silence had on his accusers?
4. Jesus was not stoned, as the first Christian martyr Stephen (Acts 7:59, 60). This was to fulfill prophecy (see Ps. 22:16, Zech. 12:10 and John 3:14, 15).

TO THINK ABOUT AND DISCUSS

1. 'We feel anger about Herod's idle wish to see the Son of God perform a miracle (v. 8); yet are there not many who view Jesus in the same way today?' Discuss this statement.
2. Pilate compromised in order to please the crowd. Can there ever be political leadership without sacrificing some principles?
3. Consider Luke 23:25. 'Barabbas symbolizes every sinner set free by the death of Jesus'. Do you agree with this statement? Give a reason for your answer.

The crucifixion (23:26-49)

As was the custom, after being sentenced, the convicted man had to carry his own cross to the place of execution. Christ, having been scourged the Roman way, would have lost large volumes of blood. All the Gospels except Luke tell of a crown of thorns placed on his head. Jesus was led away to a place where he would suffer as no man had ever suffered before.

He found it too much to carry his cross, and therefore Simon, a 'Cyrenian' from North Africa, was compelled to carry his cross. Characteristically, Jesus was concerned for others, even in the midst of his own agony and people had to be warned of judgement to come: 'Daughters of Jerusalem, do not weep for me, but weep for yourselves and for your children' (v. 28).

> The curse for their sins had been removed for ever. Atonement for sin was now complete!

Soon Jerusalem would be in ruins, and one day the earth itself would pass away. Jesus, a man without sin, was about to suffer one of the cruellest deaths known to man.

They arrived at what the Romans, using Latin, would have called 'Calvary' and the Jews 'Golgotha'. It was known as the place of a skull. There the Lord would suffer with two others. There he prayed for his enemies; 'Father, forgive them, for they know not what they do' (v. 34). It is wonderful to see our Saviour's concern for his enemies, even in the midst of such great pain.

The cross has come to be viewed as a stately and even

serene symbol—but to those living in the first century, it had very different connotations. We have to piece together several perspectives upon this manner of execution to see how the cross was viewed at that time. It was death by very slow torture. Add to that the idea of a man fastened to stocks, perhaps being ridiculed in a pillory. The cross also meant that. It held the victim in a posture which he could not change, and the crowd would ridicule him until he slipped into unconsciousness and death.

The thief knew, as did Pilate, that Jesus was innocent.

A final element to be included was that of a curse. The Old Testament taught that he who is hanged upon a tree 'is accursed of God' (see Deut. 21:22, 23 and its counterpart, Gal. 3:13). Jesus not only suffered the physical agony and ridicule of the cross, but he was *cursed* by the Father. He had taken upon himself the sins of his people. It is this inner suffering which was the hardest to bear; but which, at its conclusion, meant that his people would be blessed with every spiritual blessing. The curse for their sins had been removed for ever. Atonement for sin was now complete!

The inscription above the cross caused controversy.[15] John's Gospel tells us that the religious leaders were indignant. They wanted the inscription to read, 'He said, "I am the King of the Jews".' Pilate, however, stood by his choice of words, saying, 'What I have written, I have written' (John 19:22). The inscription—in Greek, Latin and Hebrew—was intended to be understood by all who passed by in that cosmopolitan area.

At first those crucified with Jesus urged him, 'If you are the Christ, save yourself and us' (v. 39). It is strange to consider that, if he *had* saved himself, they and all mankind would have been lost. Matthew and Mark record that both criminals rebuked Jesus. 'Even the robbers who were crucified with him reviled him with the same thing' (Matt. 27:44). Only Luke points out that later one of them came to faith in him.

The second thief rebuked the first, pointing out that the thieves were suffering 'justly' but that the Lord 'has done nothing wrong' (v. 41). The thief knew, as did Pilate, that Jesus was innocent. Next he asked a special favour: 'Lord, remember me when you come into your kingdom.' It seems surprising that the thief had the eyes of faith to see the true identity of Jesus. He knew that, even though Jesus looked helpless, he was a king. His lifestyle had been unlike that of any royal person that has ever lived. The thief could see no fine clothing (the Lord would have been naked); he could see no visible following—his friends had long since fled for their lives. His only crown, such as it was, was made of thorns. Yet the thief recognized his true identity.

He asked to be remembered by the Lord when he entered his kingdom and Jesus' reply was that even that very day he would be with him in 'paradise'. What a contrast! From excruciating pain to the refreshment of the garden of God! Such was the blessing the thief would receive that day.

Jesus dies (23:44-49)

The hours of the day were reckoned from six in the morning. We are told there was darkness from the sixth to the ninth hour; that is, from midday to three in the afternoon. Even the elements expressed the anger of the Father as Jesus took upon himself the guilt of his people. He 'became sin' for us (2 Cor. 5:21). The veil in the Temple, so long a symbol of the separation which exists between a holy God and his people, was torn in two. Matthew and Mark record that it was torn 'from the top to the bottom'. God was making a way into the holiest place, so that believers now have full access to God wherever they are (Heb. 10:19, 20)—the sacrificial system was now at an end, fulfilled in the death of the Lord Jesus. The Lamb of God had suffered, and the sins of his people were now erased.

Quoting Psalm 31:5, Jesus said, 'Father, into your hands I commit my spirit'. His work was accomplished. He could now go to the Father who, moments before, had turned his back upon his Son as he wrapped himself in the guilt of his people.

The centurion could see by the signs all around him that this was no ordinary man. Here in Luke we find him exclaiming that Jesus was 'a righteous man'. He would go on to say that Jesus was the Son of God (Matt. 27:54). Many in the crowd were similarly affected. They beat their breasts, an action symbolic of profound grief, and went away.

The burial (23:50-56)

Joseph of Arimathea was wealthy enough to have constructed his own tomb from the rock, where no one had ever been buried before. The King of kings, who had known so much poverty in his life, was now treated with dignity. John records that the body of Jesus was wrapped in two main pieces of linen, one for his head and the other for his body.

Passover was about to begin, as was the Sabbath. For this reason, even the embalming of the body of Jesus had to wait. The body was wrapped in a hundred pounds of spices (see John 19:39) and placed in the tomb. Spices and oils were prepared to be brought to the tomb early on the Sunday morning, just as the Sabbath had ended.

FOR FURTHER STUDY

1. Refer to Luke 23:34. Christ prays for his enemies to be forgiven. A similar prayer was offered by Stephen (Acts 7:60). Consider the contrast with the prayer of the Old Testament martyr, the prophet Zechariah, who cried, 'The Lord look upon it, and repay it' (2 Chron. 24:22). The purpose of the death of Jesus was mercy, rather than retribution, toward sinners.
2. Think about the words of Luke 23:34: '...for they know not what they do'. To what extent does God especially show mercy to the ignorant? (See John 9:41, Acts 3:14-17, 1 Cor. 2:8 and 1 Tim. 1:13b.)
3. Luke 23:43 mentions 'Paradise', a Persian word meaning 'walled garden'. The Lord refers to it when he addresses the church in Ephesus (Rev. 2:7). It seems that what lies before the believer is, in a sense, Eden restored. What parallels are there between Eden and Heaven?
4. Consider Luke 23:43. Some people say that the souls of those who have died sleep in the present age, and that the joys of being with God lie far ahead in the future. How far do the following texts show that heaven is the dwelling for God's people immediately after death: Luke 16:19-31; 23:43, 2 Corinthians 5:8, 9, Philippians 1:23, 24 and Revelation 6:9-11?
5. Read Luke 23:50-53. John tells us that Joseph of Arimathea was 'a disciple of Jesus, but secretly, for fear of the Jews' (John 19:38). Is it ever permissible to be a secret disciple?

TO THINK ABOUT AND DISCUSS

1. Look up Luke 23:39. 'The same happens today. People attack Jesus and rebuke him; yet they expect him to save them'. Discuss this statement.
2. Consider Luke 23:39-43. The thief who believed had no opportunity to be baptized, nor did he know much about Christ except that he was innocent and his kingdom lay beyond death. What is the minimum knowledge required for a person to be saved?
3. Note that the first recorded words of the Lord (Luke 2:49) and the last words before his death (Luke 23:46) refer to his Father. What do we learn from both of these passages?
4. Refer to Luke 23:46. In one sense the moment of Jesus' death was the voluntary passing of his spirit to the Father. How far might that be true of the moment of death for others? (See Gen. 49:33.)

24 Luke Chapter 24

The dawn rays of the sun had begun to appear on the first day of the week. More than five women could be seen making their way toward the tomb. Their names are mentioned in verse 10. Mark tells us they were concerned as to who would help them to roll away the stone. In fact it had already been moved to one side by a violent earthquake. The tomb of Jesus was empty—he had risen!

The first day (24:1-12)

The Lord told his followers that, after his death, he would rise again on the third day (Luke 9:22; 18:33 and here, 24:7). He had died to atone for the sins of his people, and risen from the dead as the 'first fruits of those who have fallen asleep' (1 Cor. 15:20).

The disciples had forgotten the Lord's words. They had been told to meet him in Galilee, over seventy miles away, after his resurrection (Mark 14:28; 16:7). Instead they remained in Jerusalem, full of grief and fear.

At the tomb, two angelic beings were present. John records

that they had sat in the tomb at the head and feet of where the body of Jesus had been. They asked a very good question: 'Why do you seek the living among the dead?' (v. 5). Furthermore, they reminded the women about the words of Christ concerning his resurrection (vv. 6-8). When the women returned to the eleven disciples, and explained what they had seen, their words were not believed (v. 11). Peter, however, felt he had to go to the tomb to see for himself. He marvelled at the sight of the linen cloths lying in the empty sepulchre. Where was the Lord?

> Christ began to give them a tour of the Bible, and teach about himself. He spoke from Moses (Genesis to Deuteronomy) and all the prophets (Isaiah to Malachi) and told them about the true identity and ministry of the Messiah. Later (v. 44) he also referred to the Psalms. If the Old Testament is not true, then Jesus was very much mistaken.

The Road to Emmaus (24:13-32)

It had been the most important day the world had ever seen. Two men were journeying from Jerusalem to Emmaus, a village which lay some seven miles away. Not much is known about these two followers of Christ—they were evidently not among the eleven disciples. They were discussing the events of the past few days. Jesus drew near to them, but their eyes were 'restrained' so that they would not recognize him (v. 16). He asked what they were discussing, and one of them, Cleopas, related the events of the Lord's life, death and resurrection. There was only one problem—he totally misunderstood the ministry of Jesus: 'We were hoping that it was he who was going to redeem Israel' (v. 21). How strange that he failed to grasp the teachings and prophecies of Jesus. The same inability to understand remains to the present day. Until God removes the veil from our hearts, we will never grasp the true identity and mission of the Saviour (2 Cor. 3:15, 16). We must pray that he will enable us to see clearly that Jesus is the Son of God, the Messiah, the one who is worthy of adoration and praise!

Christ began to give them a tour of the Bible, and teach about himself. He spoke from Moses (Genesis to Deuteronomy) and all the prophets (Isaiah to Malachi) and told them about the true identity and ministry of the Messiah. Later (v. 44) he also referred to the Psalms. If the Old Testament is not true, then Jesus was very much mistaken. He had absolute confidence in the word of God, and so should we (1 Peter 1:10, 11). How wonderful it must have been to hear the Scriptures opened up from the mouth of the Lord himself! Later, the disciples related the fact that, while he was speaking, their hearts 'burned' within them (v. 32).

As they drew near to the village, Jesus 'indicated that he would have gone farther' (v. 28). They, however, asked him to stay. As he blessed the food, it may be that something of his manner struck them that this was Jesus. Or it may simply mean that they saw the wounds in his hands (v. 39). Immediately, he vanished (v. 31). We must remember that the Lord now had a 'spiritual body' (1 Cor. 15:44) which could appear and disappear (see vv. 36, 37).

Dinner can wait (24:33-35)

Immediately Cleopas and his friend rushed back to Jerusalem and informed the eleven disciples of all that had happened. They had seen the Lord. He was alive. Mark 16:12, 13 shows us that once more the eleven were sceptical. They were not sure about the genuineness of their testimony.

Their own meeting with Christ was confirmed by Simon Peter. He, too, had seen him (v. 34). The disciples did not here mention the testimony of the women from that very morning! There must have been, however, a growing sense that something supernatural had taken place.

FOR FURTHER STUDY

1. The disciples were told that their Master would go into Galilee after his resurrection and they were to meet him there (see Matt. 26:32, Mark 14:28, 16:7). Why did they forget this clear directive?

2. Consider Luke 24:11. The Scriptures show that the first people to follow Jesus, far from being gullible, were generally sceptical about spiritual truths and demanded tangible evidence (see Matt. 28:16,17, Luke 7:19, John 14:8, 20:24, 25).

3. Why did the enemies of Jesus recall his resurrection predictions better than his own followers? Compare Matthew 27:62-64 and Luke 24:11.

4. Christ was not the very first person in history to rise from the dead. Elijah and Elisha prayed for the dead and saw them raised to life again. In the New Testament, there are many such instances (see Luke 7:11-17, John 11:38-44 and Matt. 27:52, 53). Are we prepared for the day when all who are in their graves shall rise (John 5:28, 29)?

5. Refer to Luke 24:27, 44. Jesus spoke from Moses (Genesis to Deuteronomy) and all the prophets (Isaiah to Malachi) and told them about himself. Later (in v. 44) he also spoke from the Psalms. To which passages might he have referred?

TO THINK ABOUT AND DISCUSS

1. 'Why do you seek the living among the dead?' (v. 5). Is it right for believers frequently to visit the graves of those who have departed from this world?
2. The Lord Jesus was not always recognized after his resurrection (see Luke 24:16, John 20:14-16, 21:4). With reference to 1 Corinthians 15:35-44, how different will our resurrection body be from the way it is now?
3. Consider Luke 24:27, 44. Christ had confidence in the authority of the Old Testament. Can any true child of God doubt the Bible?
4. Jesus 'indicated that he would have gone farther' (v. 28). What does this teach us about the way our Lord deals with his people?
5. Look up Luke 24:28. It is clear from Revelation 3:20 that sometimes even believers can shut the Saviour out. How important is it for us to desire his presence and open the door to him?

The disciples meet the Lord (24:36-43)

On entering Emmaus, Jesus had not asked Cleopas or his friend to invite him into a house. Here, by contrast, he appeared suddenly in the midst of his followers.

What would be his first words to them? At his arrest they had all forsaken him. He had told them to meet him in Galilee, yet they had remained in Jerusalem. However his first words to them were, 'Peace to you' (v. 36). Jesus loved them dearly, and knew how to comfort them. Mark tells us that the Lord also rebuked them for their unbelief and hardness of heart. They were rebuked for not believing those who had first seen the risen Lord (Mark 16:14).

Jesus proceeded to show them his hands and feet. He was not a 'spirit' or ghost, for he had 'flesh and bones' and, to emphasize this, he asked for food. Luke is the only Gospel writer who tells us what he ate: fish and honeycomb (v. 42, 43). A glorified body is still capable of digesting food; even angels are said to eat (Ps. 78:24, 25). The disciples must have been awestruck at the sight of their Lord and friend, now risen and eating supper in their midst.

The Scriptures opened, and further directives (24:44-49)

These verses contain three things:

HE TAUGHT THEM FROM THE SCRIPTURES and opened their understanding (vv. 44, 45). How vital it is, not only to be instructed but spiritually enlightened. Too often we stress one or the other. For this reason, scriptural teaching and preaching must be accompanied by prayer that God would open the hearts of the hearers.

HE INSTRUCTED THEM AS TO THE POINT OF THE CROSS. It brings eternal life, through the pathway of repentance and forgiveness of sins. This was to be their message to all nations 'beginning at Jerusalem' (vv. 46, 47). Christ regarded this as central to the message of the gospel.

HE TOLD THEM THAT THEY WERE WITNESSES OF THESE THINGS. Proclamation would be made, but they had to wait. He wanted nothing done in the flesh. They had been witnesses before (see Luke 9:1-6); yet for this task they would need greater help. Jesus told them to wait 'until you are endued with power from on high' (vv. 48,49).

The Ascension (24:50-53)

The apostle Paul tells us that Jesus appeared to his followers for a total of forty days after his resurrection. During that period, he taught gatherings of as many as five hundred people at once (1 Cor. 15:3-7). At the end of this time of teaching, he was to return to the Father. If ever the disciples were to receive the promised Holy Spirit in power, it had to be when Jesus had returned to heaven (John 16:7).

Jesus took the disciples up the Mount of Olives as far as the village of Bethany. Some believe that, according to Zechariah 14:1, 4, the Messiah will return to this mountain at his second coming. Certainly in Acts 1:11 the disciples were told the Lord would one day return in the same way that they had seen him leave. As he blessed his friends, he was taken from them, and carried up into heaven. No doubt this blessing included the glorious words, 'Lo, I am with you always, even to the end of the age' (Matt. 28:20). As he departed, the disciples 'worshipped him' (v. 52).

Surprisingly, Luke gives us more detail about the Ascension in his other New Testament book, The Acts of the Apostles. There he recorded that two angels were standing by as our Saviour returned to heaven. They addressed the eleven to guide and comfort them (Acts 1:11).

The eleven returned to the Temple area, as Jesus had often done; there they worshipped God. They had to wait for the Holy Spirit to come upon them in power, and equip them to serve their Master and continue his work. How long would it be before this blessing came? It was to come just ten days later at Pentecost, the fiftieth day after Passover.

We have come to the end of Luke's Gospel. To find the sequel to this book, and the magnificent expansion of Christ's kingdom in the days which followed, we must read Acts for ourselves. It is as if Luke first taught us about the life of Christ in his Gospel, and then in Acts wanted to express how his teachings may be lived out by ordinary yet transformed people, walking with God in the power of the Holy Spirit—people like Peter, Stephen, Paul and Barnabas, who lived to see the kingdom of Christ expand with breathtaking speed.

The disciples had been slow to learn, but now had come to see the purpose of the Lord's life, death and resurrection. They realized who Jesus is, and recognized the unique privileges they had enjoyed as his friends. They had not been walking with a miracle-worker only, or even the Messiah only, but with God manifest in the flesh. Here, at the close of Luke's Gospel, we leave them overjoyed in the presence of the Most High: they 'were continually in the Temple praising and blessing God. Amen.'

FOR FURTHER STUDY

1. What strange views did the disciples hold about the spirit realm? See Luke 24:37; Mark 6:48, 49; Acts 12:14, 15.

2. The empty tomb should have been enough to prove the Lord's physical resurrection, yet the disciples seem to have believed that Christ was 'a spirit'. Jesus ate food and showed his wounds because he was not a ghost but a glorified person. The bodily resurrection of all people is a vital part of Scripture teaching—see for instance Job 19:25, 26 and Daniel 12:2.

3. Jesus 'opened their understanding' (v. 45). What do sinners need in terms of guidance from others and enlightenment within if they are to be saved? (See Acts 8:30, 31; 13:48; 16:14.)

4. Refer to Luke 24:46-48. What are the main elements of the good news? How did Paul see them in 1 Corinthians 1:22, 23; 2:2?

5. Luke 24:48. The disciples were 'witnesses' of the life and resurrection of Jesus. This is a central part of the preaching of Peter—see Acts 2:32; 3:14, 15; 5:31, 32; 2 Peter 1:16.

TO THINK ABOUT AND DISCUSS

1. Reflect on Luke 24:48, 49. Why did the disciples need new power to witness, whereas in Luke 9:1-6 it seems they were already equipped for successful ministry?

2. Consider Luke 24:48, 49. How far do we ask for the power and help of the Holy Spirit today? Should we ever attempt to witness, or preach, without first asking for his aid?

3. Look up Luke 24:52, 53. For what reason were the disciples so joyful?

4. They were 'continually in the Temple, praising and blessing God'. The first Christians seem to have been good at 'continuing' in fellowship with one another, and the joyful praise of God (see Acts 1:14; 2:42, 46; 6:4; 12:5). Is the church of today characterized by such zeal?

Table 1: Events from AD 26 to AD 33

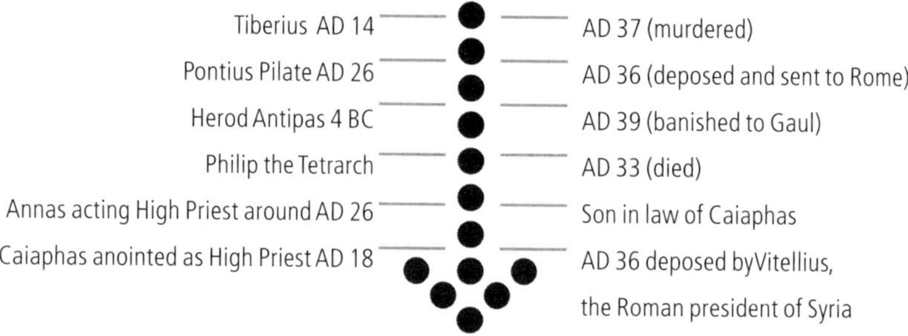

Select bibliography

John D Davis, Davis *Dictionary of the Bible*, Baker Book House, 1990.

J C Ryle, *Expository Thoughts on the Gospels*, published 1858. Re-published by Evangelical Press, 1977.

W Hendriksen, *The Gospel of Luke*, New Testament Commentary, Banner of Truth Trust, 1978.

Endnotes

1 This was a period of ceremonial washings. This lasted over forty days after giving birth to a boy and eighty days for a girl (see Lev. 12:2-5)].

2 Josephus, 'War V:5'.

3 In Deuteronomy 25:5 we learn that a man was under obligation to marry his brother's wife if he was single, and his brother dies. Herod, however, had married his brother's wife while he was still alive! Such conduct incurred the death penalty under Old Testament law (Lev. 20:10). John spoke out against Herod.

4 As there were twelve tribes of Israel in the Old Testament, so there are twelve disciples in the New. Some Bible scholars believe that the 'twenty four elders' of Revelation 4:4 represent these two groups of twelve disciples.

5 The tomb of Tutankhamen, packed with an array of breathtaking treasures, was ransacked and robbed more than once in ancient times. On at least one occasion the thieves took only the unguents (fragrant oils) and left the gold and silver. (*Treasures of Tutankamun*, p.110, ed. Gilbert, Holt and Hudson, The Metropolitan Museum of Art, 1976)

6 The Sea of Galilee is 7fi miles wide near Magdala, its widest point.

7 In the Greek, 'Tartarus'; the place of woe.

8 Beelzebub means literally, 'Lord of the Flies'. Usually the name is understood as synonymous with Satan.

9 The Pharisees were the strictest Jewish sect. Their history is obscure, but it seems they began well. At the end of the second century BC, there were strong Hellenistic influences in Israel, particularly from the incursions of Antiochus Epiphenes (175-164 BC). The Pharisees were a Jewish sect who sought to preserve the purity of worship and practice. They tried to order their lives in accordance with Scripture in every possible area. Yet their religious scruples had over time made them proud, and so blind as to miss the most important teachings of the law.

10 A silver drachma was a Greek coin, equivalent to a denarius.

11 'Mammon' is an Aramaic word meaning wealth or riches.

12 'The year before his death he told the writer of two parties for whose reconciliation to God he had prayed, day by day, for over sixty years, and who had not as yet to his knowledge turned to God…' A.T. Pierson, *George Muller of Bristol*, 1899.

13 Jim Elliott, missionary to the Auca Indians.

14 Jesus was assaulted several times before the crucifixion: before his trial (here; 22:63-5); by the Sanhedrin, by Herod's officers and twice by Pilate's soldiers: Luke 23:11; John 18:22; Matthew 27:29-31.

15 Taking the Gospels as a whole the inscription read, 'This is Jesus of Nazareth, the King of the Jews'. Each Gospel-writer gives us part of that longer statement.